D1086323

Constructions

Writing **Architecture**

A project of the Anyone Corporation

The MIT Press Cambridge, Massachusetts London, England

Constructions

John Rajchman

Second printing, 1999
© 1998 Massachusetts Institute of Technology

This book was set in Janson by The MIT Press and was printed
and bound in the United States of America.

Library of Congress Cataloging-in-Publication Data

Rajchman, John.
    Constructions / John Rajchman
        p.   cm.—(Writing architecture)
    Includes bibliographical references and index.
    ISBN 0-262-68096-3 (pbk. : alk. paper)
    1. Architecture, Modern—20th century—Philosophy.   I. Title.
II. Series.
NA680.R333   1998
724'.6—dc21   97-35756
                                                        CIP

Every truth has its historical moment.
Leibniz

If the weaver's shuttle, contrary to the proverbial stream that never flows back to its source, is a figure of the speed of passing time, then John Rajchman is a new type of philosopher. A man at the junction between two continents of thought, he personifies the stateless reason of a finite world where distances are nothing and complicity is everything—this global world of a generalized diaspora where the rapid drift of conti- **Foreword** nents of knowledge requires a *telephilosophy* of distance, the incessant transoceanic feedback of political ideals.

If indeed, in the words of Maurice Blanchot, "all presence is only presence at a distance," the presence of the contemporary philosopher of this globalization can only be situated *hinc et nunc* in an opening up and distancing of meanings. Yet this auspicious distance can be more or less wide, more or less distended. With Rajchman it attains its maximum point, for it extends from one shore to the other of our present reality, a *metageophysical* reality that closely interconnects the telecontinents of knowledges East and West while disintegrating cultures that were once precisely located.

We may recall the peculiar lever effect of the technological object called the pulley. Like the shuttle on the loom, this device also has a metaphorical dimension: a machine used to lift up, seemingly effortlessly, *what weighs down*, it is like the concept that allows *what thinks and is thought* to be released and take off. If the rapid shuttle is the perfect illustration of the constant feedback of our now globalized Time, the pivot of the pulley would then represent the axis of a Time belonging to a reason that tries to disclose the hidden meaning of the Event.

Concerned with the endgame of this pitiless century, and especially the end of a world brought about through global "teletechnologies" of action at a distance, John Rajchman's philosophy occupies the privileged space of this back and forth trajectory, from here to there, from one side to the other. Whereas ancient *metaphysical* philosophy was essentially concerned with subject and object, contemporary *metageophysical* telephilosophy is preoccupied less with Nietzsche's eternal return than its ultimate velocity. Flashback, feedback: so many unsuspected philosophical terms. . . .

"Everything is governed by lightning," said the old Heraclitus. More than two millennia later this has now been realized on a global scale! We are not so much at the end of history as at the end of the geographical world whose ancient distances of time once instigated the distancing of presence. Confronted with the transrapid "shuttle," only the transpatient "pulley" can free reason from the thunder of collective passions.

John Rajchman is thus neither a foreigner nor exactly a "traveler." He is, in the first place, a vector of the virtual space that now secretly doubles the real space of the oceans that once separated continental nations, just as day and night divided the calendar of their activities. As it was once between Greece and ancient Rome, and then between France and England not so long ago, it is now at the threshold of Europe and the Americas that the drama of knowledge and the fate of the world is being played out. Will this thought be multiple or unique? Will it be a telluric contraction or a drifting of philosophical continents of which Rajchman, something like a *Wegener*, would show us the way? Such are the unanswered questions that press urgently upon us.

Paul Virilio
Paris, 15 October 1996

translated from the French by Anne Boyman

Constructions

1

What if the architectonic in Kant were not an overarching system but
something that has itself to be constructed anew, in each case, in relation to fresh problems—something looser, more flexible, less complete, more irregular, a free plan in which things hang together
without yet being held in place? What if the Kantian
"schematism" were only a temporary construction always
to be reinvented through a free artifice no longer based
in the rules of a "productive" any more than a
"reproductive" imagination? What if we thus said
that at no time can we ever be quite sure what
our bodies can yet do, our lives become, the
shapes they might assume, the spatial
arrangements into which they might
enter—if we started from the idea   *one*   **Constructions**
that we are singular indefinite
beings, held together, prior
to anything like the uni-
fied manifold of the
Kantian "I think,"
by informal plans
that are always
departing
from
the

fixed geometries of our being, opening out onto virtual futures? What if we then, through constructions, could free the whole idea of "aesthesis" not only from the Kantian problematic of regulated faculties but also from the whole salvationist problematic of judgment or a judgment day, connecting it instead to another unfinished sense of time, peculiar to the city?

Then to think would always be to construct, to build a free plan in which to move, invent concepts, unfold a drama. Making a philosophy would become a matter of architecture in the way a novel, a painting, or a piece of music is, where the plan of construction must be always built anew, since it is never given in advance through a preset system or unbending rules. Philosophies would become free, impermanent constructions superimposed on one another like strata in a city. For once the architectonic is loosened up, the twin questions that we find in all philosophy—how to construct a work, how to construct a life—acquire new shapes. The constructed work becomes less organic, the constructed life less perfect, and the characters in the resulting drama more flexible, without univocal roles, working through provisional alliances, broken and reconciled. They then start to investigate "virtualities" unseen in the present, to experiment with what may yet happen, and constructing a philosophy becomes an art of necessarily temporary inquiry into what at a given time and place we might yet think in our thought, see or do in our visions or actions—an exercise in building new spaces for thought in the midst of things.

2

Gilles Deleuze is the contemporary philosopher who makes the most of this idea of construction; "deconstruction" is not a word in his idiom. He makes construction the secret of empiricism, the originality of pragmatism. Hume was a great empiricist because a great "constructivist," for he asked how, from "impressions," we build up a life, form beliefs, bring together our passions in the conventions of a society. He turned philosophy into an inquiry about what we may legitimately infer from such constructs of impressions, replacing the problem of certainty with that of probable belief and the question of interests and contracts with that of the particularities of passions and the credibility of governments.[1] Deleuze retains this empiricist link between philosophy as inquiry and philosophy as construction from his early study of Hume. He too thinks our lives are something like "bundles" of virtualities, with indeterminate contours, capable of entering into other possible configurations with others; and he imagines philosophy as a sort of inquiry into what happens in the resulting arrangements. From this angle he approaches the question of buildings, cities—of their dispositions. For in contrast to Heidegger, Deleuze is a philosopher not of the forest and its paths but of the city and its modes of arranging or disposing persons and things—its *agencements* (assemblages). The whole conception of building and of the philosopher as a constructor changes along with the related themes of "the Earth" and "the people" who inhabit it. The *time* of the city—of "the political"—becomes none other than the indeterminate, complex time of the possible "compositions" of our lives: a time no longer contained within given movements, natural or celestial, always going "out of joint."[2]

Alfred Hitchcock is an "empiricist" for Deleuze since he constructs a cinematic time built from relations prior to the individuals that fill them. But Jean-Luc Godard takes the idea even further in inventing a montage of "irrational continuities," where the "and" of cinematic construction falls free from the movements of the "is" of given identities or predications. Such is the great principle of Deleuze's aesthetic: a work, an *oeuvre*, is always a montage, a composition, an *agencement*. Everywhere it is always a question of construction, of architecture: a pragmatic, empiricist question always yet before us in art, in politics as in thought. That is why Deleuze thinks that "architecture is first of the arts."[3]

3

In Kant's aesthetic, architecture is the lowest, the least beau of the beaux arts because the most constrained, the most tied to money and "interests"; in it genius is fettered, unable to create "purely" or "freely," that is, on its own, from itself. It is thus the furthest from the sort of freedom enjoyed by thinking—the rational freedom of which philosophy would be the judge and protector. But toward the end of the nineteenth century we see a dual movement away from this "enlightened" idea of architecture and philosophy. On one side, architecture tries to free itself from the beaux arts, looking instead to modern engineering and industry; in place of the *maestro* of a *Gesamtkunstwerk* (as still with Frank Lloyd Wright), the architect gradually assumes the persona of an artist-engineer of the problems of modern life. On the other side, philosophy tries to rid itself of the great post-Kantian systems of thought and become "modern" in its own ways. Thus Charles Sanders Peirce starts his essay on "the architecture of theories" by declaring such systems to be in ruin. Pragmatism is his way to rebuild philosophy; he proposes an experimental empiricism with a new principle for the rules and solidarities of inquiry or the ways we come to "fix belief."[4] Thus we find a departure not only from the idea of form as the expression of "liberal" art but also of whole idea of freedom as disinterested self-legislation; freedom becomes pragmatic, experimental. Rather than trying to deliver something from nothing through the force of genius, thinking tries to construct free spaces within a terrain bounded by many constraints with the belief that things will work out in the long run. The philosopher becomes an experimenter; and as thinking becomes experimentation, its freedom lies not in pure disinterested autonomy but in the power of its constructions to go beyond what we already say, do, are to something singular or untimely. We find this idea in Nietzsche: society is an experiment and not a contract, a labyrinthine construction that we must enter and exit in many ways and by many ways, since "the way—does not exist."[5]

In this century the results of this dual turn from "genius" and "fine form" to practice and industry may be seen in the life and work of Ludwig Wittgenstein. The background is a strange intersection between philosophical and tectonic cultures that emerged in Vienna, captured in the anecdote that Adolf Loos, when it was finally arranged that he meet Wittgenstein, exclaimed "You are I!" The philosopher had become a sort of engineer, a mechanic of concepts. For while architecture freed itself of ornament and iconography, becoming pure and functional, philosophy had freed itself from the remnants of post-Kantian "metaphysics" and resolved to keep all meaning or sense within the bounds of a "logical construction [*Aufbau*] of the world," to be built mechanically from atomistic units through logical operations alone.[6] In these circumstances, Wittgenstein's *Tractatus* stands out as a work with a singular mode of construction. For it tries to show that such mechanological construction of sense becomes interesting only when we "throw away the ladder"—in effect when that logic of construction itself stops talking. Thus it points to the different idea of construction and of logic found in

Wittgenstein's later philosophy. There is a new picture. The silences of the austere "House of *Sinn*" give way to an irregular historical city whose "forms of life" must be freed from any overarching unity or completely explicit set of rules. In this city, the philosopher must construct in a new way. He confronts the new problem of what it means to follow the rules of the multiple practices that make us who we are—how, by investigating their peculiarities and variety, asked Wittgenstein, might we rid ourselves of such gross philosophical generalities as our presumption that we have "minds"?[7] These philosophical problems of "forms of life" are thus problems of a peculiar sort; and it takes a new kind of philosophical construction to explore them—a montage of overlapping and necessarily unfinished "remarks" and "investigations."

In our time Deleuze advances another, post-Wittgensteinian picture of the logic of philosophical construction. It matches not so much the industry and engineering that produced cinema as the new kinds of televisual and digital images that came to displace it: images that, no longer delimited by windows or frames, float free of vertico-horizontal space, moving instead as givens on a screen, confronting us with the question of the new arrangements of what Deleuze came to call "the brain city." According to this picture, the "city of sense" is not only disunified, defined by tacit or indeterminate rules; it is also filled with voids and interstices, always leaking and changing shapes according to its lines of leakage—such is its complexity. There is therefore a new problem: that of a potential "unregulation" or "chance" in the regularities or conventions even of "ordinary" life, which thinking must affirm through its constructions. The logic of its constructions then starts to work with informal plans built rather as montage in Godard, where one starts from "zones" in between those drawn by habit or law, drawing things together in a free virtual whole. We are presented with a new constructivism, a new empiricism, a new conception of what a work is.

4

Kant's aesthetics is preoccupied with analogies between "fine" work and "beautiful" nature, which leads to romantic or speculative notions of purposive form and organic system. But another lineage leads to Kleist and Nietzsche rather than Goethe and Hegel, in which a *Werk* is no longer an organic system developing a beautiful form, a "purposiveness without purpose." It is rather a singular, irregular construction built from many circumstances, capable of quite other stranger things than reflecting a beautiful self-accord of nature; often it knows no other logic of development than the crises it goes through. It therefore has a loose, unfinished plan before it acquires a recognizable "form" or "represents" anything, and so may be said to offer, and to be made from, "sensations" prior to forms and representations. An *oeuvre* then becomes a kind of sensation-construct of something virtual, unthought, which doesn't yet accord with anything. Such is the condition of its peculiar powers, of its anorganic vitality: it must always be unformed, indeterminate, loose enough that other figurations, other confabulations may yet happen in it or pass through it.

Deleuze makes this question of a work—of its spaces of construction and of what can yet be constructed through it—central to his aesthetic. He doesn't think the question over and done with, despite the well-documented agonies of the endgame of a reductive, purifying abstraction and the postmodern depression that follows upon it. He thinks that even "modern" works play another kind of game, *work* through another kind of abstraction. "Minor" literature, "figural" painting, "smooth" music, "time-image" film—in these cases abstraction functions not through self-referential code but through informal diagram, not by emptying all contents but by releasing other spaces, mapping other territories, not by reducing sense but by multiplying it, densifying instead of rarifying, lightening instead of purifying, complexifying rather than reducing. In such abstraction it is not a matter of architectures that refer back to their own rules of construction and nothing else. Rather it is a question of constructing free spaces of unregulation, undetermined by any prior plan, which so loosen an arrangement as to allow for sensations of something new, other affects, other precepts. It is a question of an operative abstraction working within an incomplete "virtual" architecture always to be invented anew.

5

The essays in this volume are thus each small "constructions." They try to create fresh paths or connections surrounding a question that might be put in this way: what it would mean to introduce this idea of construction into the art of building itself, into tectonic art and culture. Thus they attempt to formulate questions in, and ask questions of, a contemporary architectural practice like philosophy in a state of crisis or transmutation. For there once had been an avant-garde in architecture; it started in Europe and came to the United States, where some say it was stolen. It tried to align itself with the forces of modernization, to isolate a universal, autonomous language, applicable everywhere, that would be the pure language of architecture itself. Such was its "progressivism," its idea of "utopia," its sense of being master and possessor of the future as a "new order" of modern life. No one still thinks quite that way, yet today the reactions against it have come to seem questionable.

Contextualism has tended to an immobilizing or ersatz nostalgia; collage or superposition among existing elements has tended to a play or a transgression increasingly devoid of any virtuality, any future. Once celebrated for their complexity, context and collage became obstacles to new architecture, vehicles of the sad ironies of the post- and the neo-.

Such in any case was the impression that formed a starting point for questions that run through this volume: What would it mean to use Deleuze to introduce into this situation a new sense of "construction" neither purist nor transgressive nor utopian? What would it mean thus to put into practice an experimental art of singularizing space through informal diagrams geared to sometimes even quite small "virtual futures," which deviate from things known, inserting the chance of indetermination where once there existed only definite probabilities? How might we then be able better to see what is yet singular or untimely in the forces of our global electronic society, with its new divisions, its geographies, its dramas of worlds not quite yet ours? And what if it then happened that constructions in architecture and philosophy discovered provisional points of contact and alliance, as though together speaking a new and foreign idiom no longer belonging to the recognized languages of either?

Nothing is more disturbing than the incessant movements of what seems immobile.
Gilles Deleuze

It can happen, as in the baroque, that an architectural invention is enveloped in a larger event, implicated in a larger question that arises in our space, complicating it and our vision of it. A formal trait in architecture may then become part of the crystalliza-tion of something unforeseen with which we can only experiment or play in our seeing, our thinking, our creations. Peter Eisenman's development of Rebstockpark, a 250-acre site on the outskirts of Frankfurt, into a residential and commercial block, is about *the fold*—about the folding of architectural and urban space and also about the folding of that space into others. The fold is more than a technical device: it is the central Idea or Question of the project. But then what is a question—what is "the Question"—in architecture?

"Folding" is the name that Eisenman gives to the central formal technique employed in the generation of the design, and in this respect it plays a role analogous to that of the superpositioning of the L grid in earlier works. The nature and the scale of project, however, allow Eisenman to think in urbanistic terms. In Rebstockpark he wants to depart from the urban contextualism that rejected the modernist isolated point block or linear slab and made the perimeter block the basic unit of postmodernism. In "folding" the Rebstock plot, Eisenman would "index" complexities in urban space that have unfolded since the war and that contextualism has been unable to treat.

The starting point for the folding transformation is an imagined *Siedlung* in the prewar style of Ernst May—the once revolutionary style that supplanted the perimeter housing that the late eighteenth and early nineteenth century had carved out of the city, with what are now seen as rather corrosive effects on the urban fabric. The formal transformation then consists in successively putting this imagined design through the net of a folding operation derived from a modified version of a René Thom butterfly net. This "folding" of the complex is meant to introduce another sense of space and time within the urban landscape than that of the revolutionary tabula rasa of the modern, or the kitsch, sentimental context of the postmodern.

But this is not the only sense in which the Rebstock project is a project of "the fold." Rebstockpark is folded in many senses and many times over—many things are implicated in it or implied by it. To explicate what it implies, or to unfold what is implicit in it, one must thus unravel the general questions of space, time, vision, technology, and architecture that its Idea involves. For, in architecture as elsewhere, an Idea is never exhaustively or integrally realized in a single work; in any given case, there are always "complications." And that is why, as Leibniz knew, in explicating something it is always difficult to know where to begin and how to end.

Rebstockpark is then about folding in architecture. But what is the fold, and what it is to fold? Gilles Deleuze, in his philosophy and his reading of the history of philosophy, has developed perhaps the most elaborate conception of folds and foldings, which he sets forth in *Le pli*. The book is a study of Leibniz and the baroque, and it ends with these words: "What has changed is the organization of the house and its nature. . . . We discover new ways of folding . . . but we remain Leibnizian since it is always a question of folding, unfolding, refolding."[1]

One may say that *Le pli* is Deleuze's most architectural book, for it envisages Leibniz's philosophy as a great baroque edifice and supposes that his philosophy formulates the idea of such edifices: the idea of folds endlessly passing over into other folds, folding into folding to infinity. Yet in terms of the new ways of "folding, unfolding, refolding" that *we* continue today, Deleuze discusses *l'informe* in music, painting, and sculpture but makes no reference to contemporary architecture. We may thus regard the "folding" of Rebstockpark as Eisenman's attempt to take up the question about contemporary architecture and urbanism that these last sentences implicitly raise, discovering thereby something unnoticed, implicated all along in his own work and thought: as Deleuze invents a new philosophy of the *informe* or an *informel* art of thinking, so with Rebstockpark Eisenman invents an architecture of the *informe* or an *informel* way of building and designing.

Intensive Reading
The Rebstock project may then be taken as a reading— an "intensive reading"—of *Le pli*, and *Le pli* of it. What Deleuze calls an intensive reading is not an internal formal reading or an external contextual one but rather an experimental encounter. An intensive reading releases

unnoticed "complicities" between two spaces that remain divergent and singular or common "implications" between two things that remain differently "folded" or constituted. One example is the use that Deleuze himself makes of the passage from Bernard Malamud's *The Fixer*, which serves as an exergue for his book on the practical philosophy of Spinoza, in which an old Russian Jew explains before an Inquisition authority that he read a few pages of Spinoza's *Ethics* and then "kept on going as though there were a whirlwind at my back."[2] This "whirlwind" becomes important for Deleuze's conception of Spinoza as a "practical philosopher" and for his concept of the intensive encounter in Spinoza's philosophy. In discussing the fold, Deleuze uses the term again to describe the sort of "multilinear ensemble" through which, by intensive encounter, philosophy connects with history and with something like architecture: such foldings of philosophy and architecture as *Le pli* and Rebstockpark into one another "would be like the detours of a movement that occupies the space in the manner of a whirlwind, with the possibility of emerging at any given point."[3]

Plica ex Plica

Deleuze explains that the arts of the *informe* are about two things: textures and folded forms. The baroque invents one possibility of fold and texture: there are the textures through which matter becomes "material" and the enfoldings of the soul through which form becomes "force." In the baroque as in Leibniz, the metaphysics of formed matter is replaced by a metaphysics of materials "expressing" forces. The baroque thus opens, without prefiguring, possibilities of texture and fold later taken up in other ways by Mallarmé and Heidegger. For example, Deleuze finds that the release of garment folds

from the contours of the body shown in baroque painting and sculpture is unexpectedly continued in a different way in the mad theory of veils proposed by
Clérambault, the French psychiatrist whom Jacques
Lacan (who maintained a special affinity with the
baroque) took as his master.[4]

But there is also a linguistic point: the words
belonging to the texture and the fold family have a philosophical use and lineage, for the weaving or *plex-* words
(like *complexity* and *perplexity*) and the folding or *plic-*
words (like *complication* and *implication*) define, in modern
European languages, a family whose members include
terms like *imply* and *explain* with important places in the
philosophical lexicon. Indeed, the last words of Deleuze's
book might be read as saying, "We are still implicating,
explicating, replicating." But there is one member of this
family—whose lineage goes back to a Latin "enfolding"
of the Greek and thus to the Greek or dialectical fold—
of which Deleuze is fond above all others, and through
whose eyes he sees all the others: the word *multiple*.
Thus on the first page of his book Deleuze declares:
"The multiple is not only what has many parts, but what
is folded in many ways."[5]

A defining principle of Deleuze's own philosophy is
that the Multiple comes first, before the One. In this
sense, states of affairs are never unities or totalities but
rather "multiplicities" in which have arisen foci of unifi-
cation or centers of totalization. In such multiplicities
what counts are not the terms or the elements but what
is in between them or their disparities; and to extract the
ideas that a multiplicity "enfolds" is to "unfold" it, tracing the lines of which it is composed. Multiplicity thus
involves a peculiar type of com-plexity—a complexity in
divergence—where it is not a matter of finding the unity
of a manifold but, on the contrary, of seeing unity only as

a holding together of a prior or virtual dispersion. Complexity thus does not consist in the One that is said in many ways, but rather in the fact that each thing may always diverge, or fold, onto others, as in the ever-forking paths in Borges's fabled garden. A "multiple" fabric is such that one can never completely unfold or definitively explicate it, since to unfold or explicate is only to fold or "complicate" it again. Thus, while it may be said that for Deleuze there are folds everywhere, the fold is not a universal design or model; and indeed no two things are folded in just the same way. The multiple is thus not fragments or ruins supposing a lost or absent unity any more than its incessant divergence is a dismemberment of some original organism.

In this image of complexity-in-divergence and the multiplex fabric, we may discern one complicity between the Deleuzean and Eisenmanian folds: the Idea of a folding together, or complication, which does not reduce to relations among distinct elements in a space-time parameter but which rather supposes a strange invisible groundless depth from which irrupts something that creates its own space and time. By reference to such "intensive" complexity, the two attempt to depart at once from Cartesian space and Aristotelian place. As Deleuze puts it, "I don't like points. *Faire le point* [to conclude] seems stupid to me. It is not the line that is between two points, but the point that is at the intersection of several lines."[6]

Perplication
Deleuze, of course, is not the first to raise the question of complexity in architecture or to connect it to mannerism and the baroque. On the contrary such discussion itself belongs to an entangled historical nexus, which includes, in the first generation of the Frankfurt

School, Walter Benjamin's study of the baroque *Trauerspiel*, to which Deleuze returns in *Le pli*. But more important for Peter Eisenman's background, and for his generation, are two authors to whom Deleuze does not refer: Robert Venturi and Colin Rowe. Deleuze not only has a different view of "manners" from these authors—not a mannered decoration attached to an essential shed or habitation, but rather manners detaching themselves from a habitation no longer seen as essential, something as the flowing folds of baroque garb detach themselves from the body—but he also starts from a different conception of "complexity" itself. His is not Venturi's notion of a contradictory or "difficult" whole; it is not Rowe's image of cubist collage and Gestalt perception. For the first reduces complexity to the totality and simplicity of compositional elements, and the second reduces depth to the simultaneity of figure and ground. Thus they eliminate what makes complexity multiple and divergent and what makes depth intensive and ungrounded. They assume a bounded or framed space in which discrete elements may be associated with one another, more or less ambiguously; and so they subordinate diversity to unity, rather than seeing unity as a contingent operation holding together a potential divergence. That is why their thought leads to the sort of liberal-minded empiricist "toleration of ambiguity" that they oppose to the revolutionary-minded rationalist promise of a new order. By contrast, Deleuze's conception of complexity-in-divergence leads to the Question; it leads to the practical ethic of not being unworthy of what is disturbing the spaces we inhabit—of this Other who is knocking at our door. It involves a notion of "distance" or "distantiation," which allows Deleuze to find something baroque in constructivism, as well as in Foucault's idea that the only sort of perplexity worth pursuing is the one that takes us from ourselves.

Deleuze thus speaks not only of implication, explication, and replication but also of what, in *Différence et répétition*, he calls "perplication"—a folding through or folding across.[7]

"Perplications" are "cross-foldings" that introduce a creative distantiation into the midst of things. Such distance is the holding apart—what Deleuze calls the "disparation"—of a space that opens in it the chance of a "complex" repetition (not restricted to the imitation of a given model, origin, or end) or a "free" difference or divergence (not subordinated to fixed analogies or categorical identities). Perplications are thus what allows one to trace the diagonal lines in a fabric that cut across it so as to fold it again. They are the times of "the question," for it is just when a question comes into a space that the space discovers its free complexity; and conversely, when a space freely complicates itself it always opens itself to question. This perplexing sort of complication is thus not a matter of resolving a contradiction, as with Venturi, but rather of what Deleuze calls "vicediction" or the weaving together of a multiplicity. It is concerned with a kind of depth that is not a ground, as with Rowe, but rather the "groundless" depth of an intensive space in the extensive one that includes or frames it. Perplications thus are the foldings that expose an intensive multiple complexity in the fabric of things rather than a contradictory framed one; they unearth "within" a space the complications that take the space "outside" itself, or its frame, and fold it again. For Deleuze this deep or groundless complexity is always *virtual*—disparation is always a virtuality in a space, a sort of potential for free self-complication. But such virtuality cannot be a *dynamis* any more than such actuality can be an *energeia*; for otherwise complexity would reduce to the unity of pregiven origins and ends. "Intensity" is rather a nondynamic energy; and actuality always occurs in the midst of things, just as virtuality is always to be found in their intervals. Thus the virtual space that a line of actuality exposes in a fabric is not at all a possibility or a design to be integrally realized within a fixed frame, but rather the movement of a question that opens onto new uncharted directions.[8] That is why the times of perplication that hold a space apart are times of a peculiar sort— not times of the instantiation of eternal Forms, not times of the continuation of traditional customs, but the "untimely" moments that redistribute what has gone before while opening up what may yet come.

In such perplicational terms one may then read Eisenman's motto, reported by Tadao Ando: "In order to get . . . to a place, you have to . . . blow it apart . . . you have to look inside it and find the seeds of the new."[9] One must disparate a space or blow it apart to find the complexity of which it is capable; and conversely, the deep or intensive complexity of a space is shown in those moments that hold it apart, taking it out of itself, so that it can be folded anew. In Eisenman's words: one must make "present" in a space its implicit "weakness" or its "potential for reframing." The principles of his perplication are then that there is no space and no place that is not somewhat "weak" in this sense; and that weakness is always imperceptible, prior to the point of view that one normally has on the space or the place. Thus where architectural or urban vision for Venturi and Rowe remains a matter of discovering an imperceptible unity in a perceptible diversity of elements, in the Rebstock project it becomes a matter of "indexing" an imperceptible disparation in what presents itself as a perceptual totality.

The Rebstock Fold

What then is an "architecture of the *informe*"? One of Eisenman's words for it is "excess." An architecture of the *informe* is one that exposes its containing grid as "constraining" or "framing" something that is always *exceeding* it, surpassing it, or overflowing it. The grid has always been a central element in Eisenman's architecture and architectural discourse,[10] and in the Rebstock project it does not disappear; it is not, and cannot be, abolished. The strategy is rather to introduce something into—or more precisely, to find something "implicated in"—the gridded space, which it cannot contain, which leaks or spills out from it, linking it to the outside. In this way the grid becomes only a dimension of the folding of the space in which it figures.

Eisenman uses the term *frame* to discuss the grid, as that term has been elaborated by Jacques Derrida, notably in his work on "the truth in painting": much as Derrida says that the dream of a completely unframed space is vain (and that "deconstruction" is not that dream), so one might say that there is no such thing as a gridless architecture. Yet there exists a "complexity," or a potential for folding, that is not contained within any frame or grid; on the contrary, a frame or grid only exists within a larger virtual complexity that exceeds it. What is thus implicit in a space, which it cannot frame, may at any point or moment break out of it and cause it to be reframed. "Reframing," in other words, is a virtuality in all "framed" complexities.

For Eisenman, in the case of architecture this means that there exists something exceeding Vitruvian commodity, firmness, and delight—something that cannot be simply read as the adequation of Form to structure, site, or function but that allows Form to detach itself from such determinants and freely fold: namely the intensity that releases an "excess" that takes a space outside its bounds or through which it becomes "beside itself." The condition of the *informe* would then be that of this intensive space that seems to break out from the intervals of the articulating elements of the bounded space and the traditional place in which it occurs, with a free, smooth "rhizomatic" energy that exceeds the framing of site, plan, and program.

This cluster of ideas is then what distinguishes the folding of Rebstockpark from Eisenman's earlier attempts at superposition. Superposition still preserves the simultaneity of figure and ground and so does not yet find or invent a groundless smooth depth. In Rebstock, Eisenman starts to work instead with a type of com-plication that is no longer a matter of linear juxtaposition in an empty space or "canvas" but rather assumes the guise of a great "transmorphogenic" irruption in three-dimensional space. Rebstock is a smooth, folded space rather than a striated, collaged one and so no longer appears rectilinear or Cartesian. Thus the Idea of the project (as distinct from its program or plan) passes from a punctual dislocation of a Place to a multilinear smoothing out of a Site, and from notions of trace and archaeology to notions of envelopment and actuality—to the attempt to release new points of view or readings of the "context" that are imperceptibly implicit in it.

In Rebstockpark, the housing and commercial units no longer figure as discrete extrusions out of a planar gridded space but appear to have been deformed through an intensive *intrusion* that seems to have come from nowhere and to take one elsewhere. They appear as though they were the remains of an irruption that had broken out from the ground and returned to it, suggesting that such a "catastrophic" occurrence might again arise anywhere in the calm solidity of things.

The Rebstock fold is thus not only a figural fold as in origami—not a matter simply of folded figures within a free container or frame. Rather the container itself has been folded together, or complicated, with the figures. Rebstock is folding in three dimensions. Hence one is not dealing just with an urban "pattern"; rather the urban "fabric" on which the pattern is imprinted is folded along this line, becoming thereby more complex, more multiplex. The periphery of the plot thus ceases to be its defining edge and becomes instead one dimension of an uncentered folding movement that overtakes the site, pushing through and out of it like a sudden whirlwind.

Thus the units or their juxtaposition no longer define the spaces in between them as more or less filled voids. On the contrary, the space in between the units has come alive, for the "crease" of the fold intrudes from out of the midst of them. The crease line—an intrusive or fault line—now seems to differentiate or distribute the units in a noncontiguous continuity, where each unit becomes singular or disparate, even though it "co-implies" the others along the line. The crease is thus not a coordinating, containing, or directional line—it does not resolve an inner contradiction, establish a "difficult whole," or juxtapose figures as in a collage. It is rather a free, vicedictory line that instead of going from one point to another traces a multidimensional space, without fixed points of beginning and ending, of which one can never be quite sure where it has come from or where it is going.

The Rebstock fold is thus an intensive line, energetic without being dynamic, dimensional without being directional, but it is also a perplicational or perplectic line. It does not follow the "strong" determinations of the program, structure, or site alone but tends at the same time to take one "outside" them. For while in functional terms the crease of the fold is the connecting space between the various activities to be carried on in the modules, in architectural terms it offers the sense of the sudden emergence in the site and its activities of another free space that escapes them. It has the look of the arrested moment of an irruption whose cause is unknown or external to the site and its uses and the feel of an explosive energy that seems to come from somewhere else. Thus the fold distances one from one's habitual perception or reading of the space, as if to transport one to this "elsewhere" where things go off in unimagined directions or are folded again.

Because Rebstock is in this way folding in three dimensions, its flowing movement can not be wholly captured in a figure/ground plan. The plan is only one point of view, one aperture or opening onto a movement that, since it is "smooth," cannot be "drawn" as in a coordinated projection. Indeed Eisenman thinks that the whole relation to projective drawing changes. Folding can't be projected from a combination of plan and section but requires a topographical model and involves another kind of sign: the index. In this case the proverbial index finger points to something unseen, to a virtual movement that would not destroy the site but "reframe" it, setting it off in other directions. For the deep complexity of a site is always "implicit"—imperceptible in space, virtual in time. That is why to discover it one must "blow the place apart." In Deleuze's idiom, one might say that the index points to something that cannot be "mapped" but only "diagrammed"—the intensive space within the extensive one or the smooth space within the striated.

What Eisenman calls weak urbanism may then be defined as the attempt to provide for a moment of urban "envelopment" in urban development or to provide a place for urban diagrammatization within the space of urban planning. The idea of the Rebstock fold is to become this surface on which urban events would be inscribed with an intensive actuality. It thus involves a particular point of view on the city.

Light Regimes

One can imagine different points of view or perspectives on the city: that of the cartographic photo from the plane above, which gives the impression of a god's-eye view; that of someone who knows his own district or neighborhood so well he can see the whole city refracted in it; or that of the *flâneur*: the perspective of the Baudelairean walk or the situationist *dérive* (drift). Implicit in Deleuze is another idea: the point of view of the implications and perplications of the city. With his conception of complexity goes an art of seeing.

Folding and seeing, complexity and clarity, perplexity and illumination—it has long been asked how these go together. In Neoplatonism, the One is a Lumens Divinis, faintly shining through the complications in everything, ever waiting to be read again. Via Gershom Scholem, one can find something of this tradition in Walter Benjamin's account of baroque allegory. But in the Deleuzean multiplex, complexity is such that things can never be folded back to a first seeing, to a single source or "emanation" of Light. Rather than a god's-eye view on everything, there are only new points of view always arising everywhere, complicating things again. For light is not One but multiple : and one must always speak of *les lumières*. Illumination or clarification is thus never a complete reduction of complexity to obtain an uncomplicated or unfolded planar surface or transparency. On the contrary, in the first instance, it is the multiple complications in things that illuminate or clarify, redistributing what may be visible and what obscure.

Thus, according to Deleuze, it is just when, in Leibniz and the baroque, space becomes "folded" or acquires the sort of "texture" that can express force that there is a dual departure at once from Cartesian logic and Cartesian optics—from the regime of the "clear and distinct." There arises another "regime of light" in which things can be inseparable or continuous even though they are "distinct" and in which what is "clear" or "clarified" is only a region within a larger darkness or obscurity, as when the figures emerge from a "dark background" in the baroque painting of Tintoretto or El Greco. Thus the windowless monads illuminate or clarify only singular districts in the dark complexities of the world that is expressed in them; and Leibniz becomes a "perspectivist" philosopher for a world that has lost its center or can no longer be illuminated by the Sun of the Good.

But our own *informel* foldings involve no less a type of seeing or perspectivism, for one can never see the deep intensity or virtual complexity of a space without changing one's point of view on it. To inhabit the intervals or disparities of a city, tracing a diagonal line in its fabric, is to see the city as never before: to see something not given to be seen, not already "there." Divergences are what permit "subjective" points of view or perspectives and not "subjective" views of an unchanging uncomplicated space that permit perspectival variation. That is why Deleuze says that the "there is" of light is not given by the subject or in his field of vision; on the contrary, the subject and his visual field always depend on the light that there is. For illumination or enlightenment always comes from the midst or intervals of things; and the disparation of a space is always a kind of illumination or enlightenment. It is as if, through the crevices of the city and the cracks of its edifices, light were always seeping in, illuminating the lines of its becoming other. In its intervals and imperceptible holes, *la ville* is thus always virtually *radieuse*; and that is why the free folding of its fabric is always illuminating.

Disparate Vision

The Rebstock fold implies a peculiar sort of architectural vision: an art of light and sight whose principle is not "less is more" but "more or less than what is there." Folding is an art of seeing something not seen, something not already "there." For the jumbled lines and titled planes of the folding irruption, which deflect its surfaces onto its angular remnants, do not translate a free-flowing or transparent space. They do not possess even what Colin Rowe called "phenomenal transparency": they do not fit in a "pictorial" space where light is cast on a complex of clear and distinct forms for an independent eye standing outside their frame. Yet if Rebstock has a different feel from a free-flowing modern transparency, it is not achieved by enclosing the units and attaching to them a kitsch set of contextualizing or historicizing symbols. Rather the fold creates a different kind of "flow"—the flow of an energy that the bounded space seems to be impeding, that is spilling over into its surroundings, interrupting the calm narrative of its context and so opening new readings in it.

The heraldic and emblematic imagery of baroque and mannerist art presented visual enigmas that interconnected images and signs, seeing and reading. What Eisenman calls the index is not exactly such allegory, yet it uncovers a complexity in things, a complication prior to what is given to be seen or read or that lies "in between" the things that are seen or read: this free region where the visible and the readable are implicated in one another and the fabric folded anew. Thus, in Rebstock the eye is no longer directed, as in modernism, to an uncomplicated and unadorned space, where clarity is distinctness; it is no longer shown an "illumination" of structure and use so pure that all reading would be eliminated. But the eye is not shown a cluster of allusions to tradition, nor is its reading historicist. Rather Rebstock complicates the space in which forms might otherwise freely flow and so intrudes into its site, unfolding unnoticed implications. It works thus as an index that points to a diagrammatic rather than a programmatic or a nostalgic reading of the site—an illuminating disparation in the midst of things.

The "vision" of modernism meant a *replacement* of what was already there; the "vision" of contextualism meant an *emplacement* with respect to what was already there. What Rebstock would give to be seen is rather a *displacement* or "unplacing" that would be free and complex, that would instigate without founding, that would open without prefiguring. It is just when vision becomes multiple, complicating, and "perspectival" in this way that Hermes becomes nomadic, inhabiting the intervals and the midst of things rather than carrying messages from one place—or one master—to another. No longer content simply to reestablish the "hermeneutic" places, sites, or contexts of messages, Hermes creates his own space, his own lines of flight or creative divergences, rather as *le pli* can refer to the envelope in which a message is sent—something, of course, that facsimile transmission would dispense with.

Urban Electronics
Rebstockpark is to be the first thing one sees heading from the airport for downtown Frankfurt, now

announced by the new Helmut Jahn tower—a new gateway to the city. Once the home of a great critical-philosophical school, Frankfurt has become the finance capital and, afterward, a kind of "museum capital" of the *Wirtschaftswunder*, the German postwar economic "miracle," museum and capital having discovered a new type of interconnection and, with it, of architecture.[11] Site of a former Luftwaffe airport, a *tabula* that was literally *rasa* by the war (and that neither client nor architect find worth "recalling" in the project), the Rebstock plot is now, in the post- and post-postwar period, internationally noted for its proximity to the site of the annual Frankfurt book fair. One implication of the Rebstockpark fold is then the way it supplies a sort of contortionist vision of the whirl of this postindustrial capital of the *Wirtschaftswunder*.

Among the vectors that have transmogrified urban space, those of transport and transmission have performed a key role: in some sense it is the auto and the airplane that killed off or complexified the rational grids and the radial city of nineteenth-century industrialism. Such processes supply the starting point for the analyses of urbanist and philosopher Paul Virilio, who, like Eisenman, thinks that to understand the complexities of the city we must depart from a "static urbanism" and view the city instead in terms of the movement, rhythm, speed, in a word the "timespaces," that the various modes of transport and transmission make possible.

Along such lines Virilio proposes to analyze the intrusion into the urban environment of a "timespace" rooted in electronics technology, spread out yet interconnected through the likes of facsimile transmission and closely tied to the finance capital with which the Rebstock development is linked in so many ways. The result is what Virilio calls "the overexposed city." But if this "overexposed" city is unlike the "collage" city brought about through the transformations of nineteenth-century industrialism, it is because its complexity is not so much that of a Lévi-Straussian *bricolage* of distinct elements as of a Deleuzean texture or interweaving of disparities. The overexposed city is intensive or explosive, not gridded—a city in which incessant "movement" is prior to the apparent immobility of traditional place or planned space.

Philosophers of science once debated what it means to "see" electrons and so whether such "theoretical entities" are real or only inferred. Today everyone tacitly counts them as real, because without ever seeing them, one nevertheless cannot but "inhabit" the space of what their ever miniaturized and transportable manipulation makes possible—a manipulation that is becoming ever more direct, interactive, or "live." Toward this space, which "exposes" the city and to which it is "exposed," Virilio adopts the critical attitude of what he calls "nonstandard analysis." In the Rebstock project, Eisenman seems to adopt what might be called an attitude of perplectic analysis. For there is a sense, at once spatial and historical, in which the Rebstock site is "framed" by the railway and the highway lines that lead into the city, where museums now cluster about the old river Main, which the Franks eponymously crossed. By contrast, the electronic space in which we move and make moves "exposes" the city to something that can no longer be read as a structuring or framing network or seen through the materials and locations that realize it. For it is in itself invisible and unlocalizable; it no longer requires the sort of physical displacements that provided the sense of mobility and congestion captured in the progressivist and futurist imagination.

The energy of Rebstock is thus not a directional "dynamism" racing toward a sleek new future; rather it belongs to a sort of irruptive involution in space; and this multilinear nondirectional energy takes one out of the traditional gridded city. Rebstock gives neither a futuristic nor a nostalgic sense of our electronic moment but an "actualist" one. Its attitude to the new electronic technologies is neither rejection and nostalgia nor the manic embrace of a California cybercraze. It is rather an attitude of this perplexity of the multiple "elsewhere" that the technologies introduce into our ways of inhabiting spaces. Rebstock is not about the arrival of a new technological order anymore than it illustrates the postmodern sense that nothing can happen any more, that all that will be already is, as though history had come to an end in the self-satisfaction of the health club or the shopping mall. It is rather about this implicating, explicating, replicating energy that is always escaping or exceeding the space and the locale in which it is implanted, introducing a distance that allows one to look back upon the gridded or collage city with the mixture of nostalgia and horror with which one once looked back *from* it to the country.

Perhaps one might thus speak of a new relation between architecture and technology. The Bauhaus sought to display in architecture the preelectronic industrial engineering that had made possible a whole new program of "rational" building and construction, artist and engineer joining in the new figure of the architectural *Gestalter*. But "postindustrial" electronic technology shows itself architecturally in a different manner: in terms of a free excess in formal variation that still remains compatible with structure and use and that is made possible by invisible means. It is shown in an exuberant detachment of form, in the sort of the contortions between the random and the regular that electronic modeling makes possible. Thus from the Bauhaus aesthetic of geometric abstraction one passes to the electronic aesthetic of "free" abstraction, where an intensive line goes "all over," released from its subordination to the grid—a passage from formal juxtaposition to *informel* smoothing out, of the sort Deleuze associates with Klee rather than Kandinsky, in the points, lines, and inflections of the Bauhaus painters.

Metroplex

We thus inhabit the metroplex. There is no completely rational space, no completely adequate place, and the alternative between topia and utopia no longer defines our possibilities. That is why the Rebstock style is neither "international" nor "regional," "elitist" or "populist," but rather moves in a space in between. While it always remains "now-here," it seems to come from "nowhere," for, in the words of Deleuze, while there are folds everywhere, the fold is not a universal design. Rather, singular or new foldings somewhere in the social fabric provide the chance for the emergence of this *peuple à venir*, this "people-to-come," that is no longer identified by a rational space or an adequate place, of which Deleuze declares the architect always has need, even if he is not aware of it.

Deleuze presents the baroque as marking a moment when the collapse of the old heliocentric *cosmos*, where man imagined he had his place and his task, gives rise to a decentered perspectival *mundus*, where each monad has a particular point of view on the world it includes or expresses—the moment when the traditional separation into two different realms is replaced by a single edifice with two stories, in which there is a "new harmony" between an enclosed interior and an inflected exterior. But our own "foldings" no longer transpire in such a baroque *mundus* any more than in an ancient *cosmos*, for "the organization of the house, and its nature" have changed. Our manners of coexistence can no longer be held together through the principle of the baroque house—the greatest or most complex variety in a single compossible world—for the world we inhabit is multiplex. We no longer have—we no longer need to have—the good cosmos or the best world, the illumination of the form of the good or the clarification of the principles of the best. Our foldings, our own "mannerisms," have dispensed with the single best world, turning rather to the complicities and complexities of the disparation through which things diverge into others; our invention of new "manners" of being comes in response to events that disrupt our contextual frames, complicating things again, introducing new enfoldings, or free spaces of implication. From the good city and the best world we have passed to an intensive cityspace or metroplex, where we are no longer supposed to find the identity of context or of reason, of tradition or eternity, but are free instead to practice an art of inhabiting the intervals, where new foldings arise to take our forms of inhabitation in new and uncharted directions. And so, in the place of the cosmopolitan or universalist thinker, "citizen of the world," there arises a strange, new, ubiquitous nomadic community of *metroplexed* thinkers, perplectic inhabitants of our contemporary "chaosmos."

Games of Chance

What then is "complexity," what is "the question" in architecture today? In the drama of philosophy, Deleuze finds the invention of various philosophical protagonists: there is Hume, the inquirer, or Kant, the judge at the tribunal of reason. In *Le pli*, Leibniz figures as the defense attorney of God, a great inventor of "principles" in philosophy, a whole Jesuitical jurisprudence to account for the incessant emergence of perplexing cases. Leibniz was the genius of principles, and the principle of Leibnizian jurisprudence was inclusion in the best world that God selects, and that, in some sense, we ourselves are "inclined without being necessitated" to select, even though that means that some of us must be damned. Deleuze calls Leibnizian principles "cries of reason" in the baroque world that theology seems to have deserted.

But as we today in our "post-Enlightenment" times find a multiple intensive complexity in things prior to simplicity and totality of compositional elements, the perplexing case—the question—acquires a positive capacity to reframe or recreate our principles, our jurisprudence itself; and there emerges a new type of player in the game of the complexities of thought. Deleuze sees Nietzsche as announcing a new protagonist in philosophy, one who starts to play the game in the new way given by the two Whiteheadian principles that Deleuze makes his own: the abstract or the universal is not what explains but what itself must be explained; and the aim of the game is not to rediscover the eternal or the universal but to find the conditions under which something new may be created. In our folding, unfolding, and refolding, we no longer inhabit the two-story baroque house, where, on the heights of the windowless walls of the interior, would be heard the elevating reverberations of the cries of Beelzebub below. For complexity no longer occurs within a house governed by the principles of such an "elevating" illumination but rather becomes a matter of a multiplex play at once within and without the house—of this *pli*, this "folding," which is a matter of an inexplicable chance, prior to principles, prior to design, yet always virtual in them. The figure of our post-baroque or *informel* complexity is thus a player—the player of the new game of perplication.

It would seem that Eisenman tries to introduce just this sort of game into architecture and into architectural discourse, for, anterior to yet inseparable from the requirements of the program and the site and the space of the drawing plan, Eisenman discovers the play of the idea or the question. His architecture plays a game where chance becomes an inextricable part of design, and not something design must master or eliminate—a game whose object is to maintain the play of chance within the space of design. Deleuze distinguishes two ways of playing the game of chance. Pascal, in his wager, exemplifies the bad way, where the game is played according to preexistent categorical rules that define probabilities and where one calculates gains and losses. The true player (like Nietzsche or Mallarmé) does not play the game in this way. Rather the table itself bursts open and becomes part of a larger, more complex game that always includes the possibility of other new rules; and to play the game one must thus, in making each move, affirm all of chance at once. Thus a game of "nomadic" or "smooth" distributions replaces a game of categorical or striated ones; and chance itself ceases to be tamed or hypothetical and becomes free and imperative. It is then this free multiplex game of chance that the Rebstock fold tries to play in urban and architectural space.

The baroque fold, for Deleuze, is unlike the oriental fold, which weaves together or com-plicates empty and full spaces, voids and presences. For in the baroque, "holes" only indicate more subtle foldings, and the principle is that there are no voids, that everything is included in a single expressive continuum, as in the principle of the Leibnizian best that the greatest number of folds be fit within the same compossible world. Thus Derrida once wrote that Leibniz's God, in selecting the best world, experiences nothing of the anxiety of the Jewish God, who must create out of nothing, out of the void; and that baroque plenitude is thus symptomatic of an avoidance of the "pure absence" that a Mallarmean sort of writing would suppose and that would be incompatible with anything like a "built visible *architecture* in its locality."[12] Yet the free play of chance that Eisenman's Rebstock fold tries to introduce in design is not a "pure absence"—not a lack or void from which everything would have come. It is rather the virtuality in a space of what is "more or less than what is there," of something that exceeds the space and that it cannot integrally frame. As Deleuze remarks, "to speak of the absence of an origin, to make the absence of an origin the origin is a bad play on words. A line of becoming has only a midst."[13] In the perplication game, untamed chance is not a place, not even a void or absent place, but rather the virtual space of the free line in the midst of things.

The supposition of the game in Eisenman's perplicational architecture is thus not "absence" but "weakness"— the complex chance of a space to be folded, unfolded and folded again. In this sense Rebstock remains a "full" space—it is "full" just because it is weak, or is "filled by" its weakness. For the fold, which fills up the space, is at the same time what takes the space out from itself, bursting it open and smoothing it out, releasing an intensive energy that is neither theological nor mystical, neither baroque nor oriental, neither elevating nor quieting. Rebstock is rather "full with" a "distantiation," an unsettling question that clears out a space offering the chance of a complex repetition or a free divergence. It fills its space in a manner different from the baroque and from the checkered pattern of voids and presences defined by the modern slab or *Siedlung*—through the intervals of which a new *lumière* peers, from an intensive depth prior to figure and ground, and with a diverse complication that spills over into history and context with a perplexing tension. That is what Eisenman calls "presentness." Presentness is the splendor of the fold in the house we have come to inhabit, where the game of creation is played not *ex nihilo* but *ex plicatio*.

**A
Concept
in
Architecture**
What
is
it
to
introduce
and
try
a
new
concept?
To
try
it
out
in
architecture?
And
through
an
architectural
tabloid
such
as
ANY?
And
in
particular,

three   **Lightness**

this concept—the concept of lightness. What is lightness as a *concept*?

Simple analogy provides a restricted relation between concept and design. To try out a concept is to risk another freer, more mobile, more experimental sort of relation, where a concept is not shown in a single formal trait or signature but assembles and reassembles many different design features past and present in an original manner, linked to a larger complex that looks to architectures yet to come. So it is with the concept of lightness attempted here.

For example, Rem Koolhaas may be said to create a sense of lightness in various ways. In his Bibliothèque de France project, translucent screens establish a sort of luminous cavity in which, in apparent indifference to structure or function, certain volumes are seen to float; at the same time, a distribution of loads allows greater freedom on the bottom, as though this very large structure were bottom light—lightness as a release from load structure. A different strategy can be seen in the feeling of flight of his lean, corrugated bird—the *ava* of the Villa dall'Ava—with its thin dancing columns below and pool alighted on top, which aligns itself (and those who float in it) with the old industrial Eiffel Tower. Then there are strategies, as in the Jussieu Library project, where the script of internal conveyance by stair or escalator, glimpsed from without, floats free from the structure of its container (unlike the elevator in *Delirious New York*), endowing even the most minimalist enclosures with a strange sense of unlimited weightlessness. Or again there are the topographic research and flexible programming that free one from reading ground as base, as with the tilt of the Rotterdam Kunsthal.

A sense of weightlessness—of making the earth seem light—can be obtained in yet other ways. Some recent Japanese work is dense with talk about it, linked to a vision of the space of the new electronic Japan. Toyo Ito, for example, has tried to go beyond the dichotomy between abstract and regional spaces to discover more flexible, nomadic strategies than those promoted by an older critical regionalism. Yet another view comes from Bernard Cache. Here, release from the weight of a typological view of context is obtained through a topological conception of singularity and continuous variation, yielding an almost cinematic sense of movement prior to the traditional static collage of up-down frames. At the same time these various strategies of lightness let us see older architecture in new ways. In *Earth Moves*,[1] Cache revisits folding in the baroque and a related philosophical discussion of mind, body, and world, and so the *teatrum mundi* in which architecture starts to dance. And as Stan Allen shows, we can also see the late work of Le Corbusier with new eyes, notably the Carpenter Center at Harvard University and especially the Philips Pavilion for the 1958 Brussels world's fair, where, through the work of collaborator Iannis Xenakis, engineering and music found a common notation that undoes the dichotomy between brute simplicity and organic expressivity.

A concept thus has an open-ended relation to design. It tries to free a new complex, which serves, as it were, as a "strange attractor" to certain features or strategies, assembling them in new ways. To do this it must itself become complex, inventing a space of free connection to other concepts. "A concept is never simple," Jean Nouvel says, taking up in architecture a phrase from Deleuze. It connects others in a kind of force field that serves to displace the current *doxa*, stimulating thinking to go off in other directions or inviting one to think in other ways.

In the case of lightness this "thinking otherwise" appears as a displacement of the function of the concept, as it occurs in earlier problematics that identified lightness with immateriality. In modernism lightness was used to make a brutal break from the weighty materials of traditional masonry and context through the medium of glass and transparency. In postmodernism lightness came to express instead the disappearance of the anchoring of place, region, or proximity in the new technological world-city of postindustrial capitalism. But lightness can be conceived in other terms and so discover new functions. For one can well imagine a lightness quite compatible with matter, working through materials and textures themselves belonging to a haptic rather than an optic space.

Schopenhauer thought of architecture as an art of burden and support, an art of the spirit of gravity, at the antipodes of music in the representation of the will. Its most perfect realization lay in the columns and entablature of the Parthenon, a classical perfection later lost in Christianity with the barbarity of the crystal of the Gothic cathedral. Gravity (and so lightness) would thus be best shown in a static, delimited comparative space. To rethink lightness is to imagine another sort of space than the classical, which defines gravity in relation to vertical elevation. Lightness may then be thought of as a *release* from the traditional burden-support space of architecture.

When conceived in this way, lightness discovers all sorts of new connections. Some lie in the dynamic models of the nomadic traditions in science and mathematics, described by Deleuze and Guattari, where *gravitas* is seen in relation to *celeritas*. These allow one to describe weight or burden in contrast to speed, and speed in contrast to a static, upright coordination of space. Thus one can say that "the force of gravity lies at the basis of a laminar, striated, homogenous and centered space; it forms the foundation for those multiplicities termed metric or arborescent, whose dimensions are independent of situation and are expressed with the aid of units and points (movements from one point to another)."[2] By contrast, speed no longer refers to relative velocity of movement in such a space; rather it describes another, more disparate, lighter kind and space of movement. The two types of movement thus match two kinds of space, one delimited and comparative, the other unlimited and "disparative"; and they may then be seen in what, in the architecture of music, Pierre Boulez called striated space and smooth space.

In forging links with such nomadic conceptions in science, lightness also finds connections with the arts and, in a singular way, with the departure from verticality and frontal vision, which Michael Snow, for example, exploits in film and which Rosalind Krauss has explored in a whole new way in relation to sculpture, painting, and photography in terms of the formless. Thus one finds new ways of thinking of the relation of the spirit of gravity to the wall and the floor, which recurs in choreography and, in particular, in the choreographic attempt to show the architecture of music in movement, as in the baroque, later in Balanchine, and today with Mark Morris.

Through such connections the concept of lightness then starts to take on a new function, quite different from those that identify it with immateriality or transparency. One might think of Jacques Derrida as formulating this function when, referring to Nietzsche's "choreography," he speaks of the space and time when innocence and dance become one and the same. "The dance changes place and above all changes *places*."[3] The new role that lightness has to play goes with a new, more rhythmic conception of our very ethos. Ethos is no longer, as in Heidegger's architecturally suggestive etymology, to be thought of as a place of dwelling, any more than it is something that could be completely planned or manifested in transparent immaterial geometry. Rather our ethos consists in our multiple manners of being and how they are woven together; and in such manners there always lies the possibility of light movement in formless space, prior to both the material assignation of place and time and the immaterial mastery of space and form. The function of lightness thus is found in a certain ease or freedom in movement.

"Our whole research is ultimately about, let's say, finding freedoms," declares Rem Koolhaas—freedom from structure, from typology, from ideology. The aspirations of the '68 generation would appear in this quest, aspirations often ending in impasse, in the inability to build anything at all, in laments for the lost heroism of utopian modernism. For what is it to free space? Is it to impose, dissolve, or invent order? And what is free in making things? Is it exploding, dismantling, undoing, opening, or letting be? Koolhaas's way is a light way, unlike some of the more chaotic, explosive, or dislocating ones of his generation: lightness as the release of a freer space from the unnecessary loads that tradition asks us to bear. It is an inventive, mobile lightness that would invert the priority of critique with respect to experiment in the traditional ideological vocations of architecture: "Like a mountaineer," says Koolhaas, "who has to travel light to get somewhere . . . the advantage of a non-academic position is that we can experiment . . . even on ourselves . . . as they say in Japan: it floats."[4] This is then a lightness of the concept—of untimely experimentation in theory.

Bernard Tschumi proposes another related contemporary view of the function of concepts in architecture.

A concept is a tool that fits with others in a box, he says, reclaiming Foucault's adage for architecture itself. But if concepts are tools in a box, they do not have the sort of instrumentality or instrumental reason from which first Kantian idealism and later critical theory recoiled, finding instruments to be too caught up in material considerations, as with Kant's lowly placement of architecture in the system of the beaux arts. Rather, concepts are tools that one uses in an experimentation that is light or free, just when it exerts another sort of function than that of the given instrumentalities of program, when it releases another kind of space, opens another kind of time. One might say that the image of technique or machine itself changes as the concept becomes experimental: instead of the old modernist figure of the engineer and the mechanical order, one starts to think in terms of the inventor and experimentation with other possibilities. One no longer sees freedom (or free space) as an escape from materiality to another, higher world but as a release of other freer spaces in this one—a *lightening* of space for which one requires special conceptual tools.

A century ago Nietzsche tried to introduce the figure of the *Versucher*, the attempter or experimenter, into philosophy, connecting it to a new spirit of lightness elaborated in the story told in *Thus Spoke Zarathustra* in which the earth is renamed the light or, in the words of wisdom of the weightless bird (this other *ava*) at the close of Book III: "Behold, there is no above, no below! . . . Are not all words lies to those who are light? Sing! Speak no more!"[5] Will a certain lightness in architecture let us read those words today anew?

What then does it mean to try out a concept like lightness in architecture? Let's say that it is the question of the kinds of uses to which it can be put and to which it gives rise: the free experimentations that it helps to make possible.

The Earth Is Called Light

In 1934, in a lecture entitled "The Origin of the Work of Art," Martin Heidegger renames the earth. He steps back from modern science and uses the craft of thought to say how the Earth figures in our existence, how it shows itself in our being. The word *earth* is no longer to be understood in a way "associated with the idea of a mass of matter deposited somewhere, or with the merely astronomical idea of a planet." Instead it speaks of a "native ground"—the ground "on which and in which man bases his dwelling." "We call this ground the *earth*," declares Heidegger.[6] His lecture is about an original sense in which the work of art—painting, monument, or poem—discloses this nonplanetary native ground to us, lets it come forth and manifest itself.

According to Heidegger, the earth shown in the work of art is shown through a *herstellen* not an *ausstellen*—a setting forth, not a setting up. It is unlike anything that might be set up and exposed in a museum, shorn of its origins or "native grounds." The earth on which we base our dwelling and from which we come is, as it were, unmovable and "site-specific"; it has no "exhibition value" (*Ausstellungswert*) in Walter Benjamin's term from the same period. Resistant to exhibition, it is rather the name of a "poetic" gift or endowment of a people, a *Volk*. And when the work of art, reduced to a mere object of "aesthetics," enters the museum or is exhibited in its space, Heidegger says that it dies—as Hegel had foreseen when he told of the ending or dying of art. For the way we "dwell" on the ground of the Earth is poetic; and our poetry is what always speaks of this dwelling and this Earth. That is why the

Earth matters not only in the origin of the work of art but in the origin of its very concept, and hence in the concept as well as the work of architecture. It is well known that under this new name (which is at the same time a very old name), the Earth clears a path in Heidegger's woods that opens onto a renaming of *building* in a sense more "original" than any mere "art or technique of construction."

But Heidegger was not the only phenomenologist in 1934 to try to go beneath the merely astronomical idea of a planet and rename the earth. We find such phenomenological "geo-logy" as well in notes that Edmund Husserl was taking that same year—written, he puts in the margins, "in the midst of painful disturbances."[7] Husserl wants to extract the idea of the earth from the "natural attitude" that comes from European science and think of it instead as an original *ground*, constituted by our corporeality and our "flesh." Understood in this manner, the Earth would be prior to the astronomical body that Copernicus had in mind when he said that the earth moves around the sun rather than the other way around. Unlike such a planet, the Earth, in its "original" meaning doesn't move at all; it is still in an absolute way, prior to all relative rest or motion. It is as if we carry this Earthground around with us wherever we go and whatever we do. For even when all the parts of our body are in motion, our flesh remains tied to it; our incarnation supposes it. It stays with us when we are speeding above the ground in an airplane and would subsist even if we were to take up residence on the moon. It is what makes us all "terrestrial beings"—our common *archē* and home, the same in all our particular histories, across all our divisions and boundaries. There is one humanity as there is one Earth, Husserl writes to himself. By absolutely not moving, this original—and "universal"—ground anchors us. It centers us. It orients us in a perspective view of distances. It links oculo- and motor into a single unified kinesthetic field with receding horizons, which permits us to place things in a coordinate space, reidentify objects, and say what's up and what's down; and it makes all the textures of our *haptisch* space come to conform to this *optisch* organization. Husserl's phenomenological Earthground is thus what remains stationary in the visual field of our upright posture: as such it becomes the source of the relations between figure and ground, background and foreground, center and periphery, which supply the experiential conditions of all geometry and all European science. We must rediscover precisely such original conditions in order to emerge from the crisis into which the "natural attitude" of this science has plunged us. That is why we must learn to rename the Earth.

It is very striking today to look back from these phenomenological views or senses of the earth to Zarathustra. For he too talks of renaming the earth. He tries to teach us how to call it *die Leichte*, the light or weightless one. His alpha and omega is that "everything become light, every body a dancer, all spirit a bird." More precisely he says: "He who will one day teach men to fly will have moved all boundary stones; the boundary stones themselves will fly up into the air before him, and he will rebaptize the earth—'the light one.'"[8] But this is a very peculiar baptism, which the later phenomenological ones permit us to see from a certain angle.

One is immediately struck by this difference, that the earth is not renamed as a "ground." Indeed it is just when it is *not* taken as ground that the earth may be called "light." This alone alerts us to a different sense of building and rebuilding than the ones from the "utopian" times of the 1930s. For this earth is not a ground zero, and to discover it, we must attempt many ways or paths at once, since, as Zarathustra puts it, *"the way—does not exist!"* Nietzsche's book may itself be said to be "built" and to tell of "the earth" in such a many-wayed or labyrinthine manner.

For Zarathustra and in *Zarathustra*, the earth is not "ground" in several senses. It is not Husserl's original "arche-ground" of a flesh that centers, orients, and frames all our experience, prior to geometry and physics; it is not a ground of figures, does not "originally" divide up into foreground and background, is not defined by receding optical horizons. For the earth can not be delimited by boundary stones (*Grenzsteine*); it may even be said to be unlimited, uncentered, formless. There is *weightless* flight only when "there is no above, no below!" (*es gibt kein oben, kein unten!*), when the earth is no longer defined by being "under" or beneath the Sun, as in Plato's tale where the soul learns to reorient itself and fly out from the cave, or in other earth/sky, heaven/hell, elevation/debasement stories. Rather the earth becomes light when one can say, "The middle is everywhere. The path to eternity is crooked," and when, instead of learning to "orient" itself upward, the soul learns to trace another light sort of movement, a multiple displacement along the surface, a sort of dance. For the earth is heavy (*schwer*). But to fly is not to remain above this heaviness or gravity, as though we were to live in houses on stilts. It is to know how to *lighten* the earth itself, as though one were to insert oneself into it like a surfer in a wave.

The earth of which Zarathustra speaks is not a ground in another way as well. It is not the site of a dwelling; it is not the grounds in which "dwellings" put their roots or from which they arise or which comes forth in commemorative poetry or monument. It is not the "native grounds" of a people or a region shown in its manner of building. On the contrary, before the earth can be called "light," all boundary stones must be sent flying out into the air. Another name for "the light One" might thus be "the deterritorialized one"—the *absolutely* one.

One becomes a "native" of this earth only when one knows how to "move places," when one becomes the sort of being for whom regional boundaries make the earth seem heavy and immobile. To rename earth as "the light one" is to learn to move across such boundaries as though one were living in another, freer space. The earth may then be said to be where all those come from who as yet have no "word" to name their dwelling place and who stammer when they talk of themselves or what they are in the process of becoming. It is the earth of this people, as yet nameless and invisible, who comes out from "nowhere," gathering together to form another earth and another sense of "earth"—the earth as other possibilities of life, too strange and multiple to be total-ized in the model of the *cosmos* or harmoniously expressed in a *mundus*.

So the earth must be renamed. But how did it ever become thought to be so "heavy?" A "spirit," a *Geist*, is responsible, a spirit that Zarathustra takes as his arch-enemy, the devil who tempts him to search, making him a *Versucher* (an experimenter or attempter): the spirit of gravity. This spirit has induced us to *call* the earth heavy, determining what we think of as above and below, over and under. That is why renaming the earth is such a complicated affair, requiring Zarathustra to speak only of "he who *will one day* teach men to fly" and to declare that *all* words are too "heavy,' that all words are "lies to those who are the light." For the fight with the spirit of grav-ity is a fight over the word *light* and the word *earth*. Who besides Zarathustra calls the earth light and the light earthy? Yet that is how we must talk if we are to learn to *fly*. Who has ears to hear this song? When Zarathustra, the light or laughing prophet, the one to give this odd philosophical opera its name, sings of rebaptizing the earth, he is alone, singing to his own ears, to an empty house, for a people that has yet to invent itself. Zarathustra's house is yet to come.

Light Matters

Architects often understand lightness as *immateriality*. But can we speak of another kind of lightness that complicates and displaces this familiar understanding? Can we talk about a spirit of lightness capable of moving in even the most "heavy" brute materials and of showing even the thinnest transparencies to be slow or weighed down? Can we speak of light materialities and heavy transparencies, a strange weightlessness of the earth itself?

When masonry walls were replaced by steel skeletons and reinforced concrete, the old principle of "load and support," which Schopenhauer had taken as definitive of architecture, no longer seemed quite so essential. Buildings didn't have to be seen as holding things up from the ground or base. But this new sense of lightness was at first articulated by glass and other sorts of transparency and so came to be identified with immateriality. Thus in 1914, in *Glass Architecture*, Paul Scheerbart spoke of using glass to "dematerialize" architecture; he dreamed of whole cities floating on water ever rearranging themselves in new patterns, and so may now be said to anticipate some contemporary Japanese notions of floating, taken up in another original way in Rem Koolhaas's talk of "the lite." In these contemporary cases, glass and transparency seem much less important, and translucent skins much more frequent.

The modernists of course also used glass to get "light"; they had the famous stricture of displaying structure. They dreamt of a "light and airy" sense of space, no longer tied down to traditional "heavy" materials, ruled instead by the new morality of the clear and transparent. Their light space would be free-flowing, open, and unencumbered by traditional earthy materials; but it was also a classical space, whose clean mathematics and types of transparency Colin Rowe would later describe—an *optisch* rather than a *haptisch* lightness in the terminology of Alois Riegl, later developed by Deleuze. The modernists thus endowed lightness with a sense of time—a brutal breaking away and floating free from the "heaviness" of traditional context.

There would arise other hostile attitudes to this immaterial sort of lightness in architecture. Some are conceptually encapsulated in an impressive exhibition in Paris curated by Jean-François Lyotard in 1985, called "Les immatériaux" (The Immaterial Ones), though, of course, many of the ideas can be found earlier and elsewhere, notably in Marshall McLuhan. The focus is on the new electronic or postindustrial technologies and the global postcolonial informational and consumer capitalism that drives them. These new technologies reputedly bring about a vast process of dematerialization and deterritorialization—a loss of proximity, locality, centralization; nothing seems real or locatable anymore; everything is "floating." As with the earlier, industrial modernism, immateriality and lightness thus signify independence from context or locale. But now they have acquired a bad name. We are told that we must get back to the earth and its stabilizing "gravity"—how can we "anchor" ourselves and become Newtonian again? There is a return to a phenomenological notion of the earth as "grounds" of things; the heaviness of Tadao

Ando's concrete is seen as a great critical-regionalist challenge to the abstract transparency of global capitalism. In this way, gravity and materiality return as critical arms to combat a postindustrial weightlessness induced in our dwelling when deprived of its original rootedness in the Earthground.

Today we confront a somewhat different question. It is not a matter of the Earthground and of the weight and materiality of tradition, region, or context. It is rather a question of another conception of the earth itself and of its materialities, no longer separated from the city or caught in the opposition between artifice and nature—the question of a new "geo-logy," where the earth is no longer seen as what anchors or grounds us but as what releases in the midst of our multiple material manners of being other light, dynamic spaces.

Then how different the transparent, immaterial lightness of classical modernism looks! It seems so static; it can't *move*; doesn't float or fly. It is obtained in a negative way through a rarefaction or purification of any unnecessary materiality. It is as if lightness has been *immobilized*, enclosed in a glass house where it is required to be pure, clear, clean, without any excessive ornament. Lightness becomes optic and geometric—a bride stripped bare rather than a dethreaded Ariadne who puts a clever "yes!" into the ears of the bull moving lightly along the surface of things. A truth exposed rather a multiple possibility released.

There would be reactions against this static, unornamented lightness. Various kinds of "gravity" would pull the classical denuded bride out from her glass house to discover the earth beneath and around her, challenging the vertical-horizontal space of her optical enclosure. Lightness is asked to "come out"—out from the grid frame of its glass house to move in a freer space, where other possibilities of release from tradition exist than that of "rising above" all materiality and context. It is asked to come out and invent another kind of *abstraction* than that of the immaterial geometric form—the light abstraction of assemblages that take one out from the gravity of locales and regions, bases and heights, releasing another more disparate movement no longer content to pass from one point to another. Thus lightness might undo its long identification with immateriality and transparency in architecture and find a new concept, no longer opposed to that of the earth.

Dancing and Building

"Dancing and building are the two primary and essential arts. . . . and in the end they unite." So writes Havelock Ellis, the noted sexologist, in his book *The Dance of Life* (1923). These two arts were the first, in different and eventually overlapping ways, to call themselves "postmodern" and then move on, as though they shared a special sense of the changing spatial configurations. They had already been united in modernism, as exemplified in the figure of Rudolf von Laban, with his ties to the Bauhaus; and each had relations with the new art of cinema and what Deleuze analyzes as its "movement images." Laban's notation offers a sort of graphics to "see" something of their shared modern configuration of space. Perhaps today the mathematical models proposed by René Thom allow us to see other configurations, for these "dynamic" models depart from static, coordinate analytic geometries and their discrete points.

Dancing and building are also the two arts most directly concerned with gravity. "Everything is gravity," says Mark Morris. But of the two, dance has been the most constantly associated with the lightness that serves as an antidote to a melancholy immobility, as in the case of Nietzsche, but also, for example, in the poetry of John Donne. The question is rather *how* gravity figures in dance. Laban's student Mary Wigman wrote about the problem in 1933, speaking of how "our technical age" had engendered a "dance-motivated being," a rhythm behind the motor, shown in a cult of "body consciousness," which was replacing a lifeless, formalized ballet: "The ballet-dancer developed an ideal of agility and lightness. He sought to conquer and annihilate gravitation. He banned the dark, the heavy, the earthbound, not only because it conflicted with his ideal of supple, airy, graceful technique, but because it also conflicted with his pretty aesthetic principles."[9] That was before the discovery of the floor, by Martha Graham, among others. Part of what made ballet "classical" was that its space was delimited by centers of gravity, with horizontals defining the verticals of the falls and with movement going from one point to another. Graham opens the horizontal toward the Earth beneath; bodies can barely get up from the floor, from where the most dynamic movements arise, as though it is only when the body is no longer upright that it can discover the "earthy" energies of contract-release.

Today Morris offers another sense of lightness. He *plays* with tradition rather than *bearing* it as a load, unconcerned with the problem of "the end of dance" or with the proposition that dance is movement of any sort. He invents a choreography of disparity and connection, shown in a multiplicity of costumes, movements, genders, and the "levity" that comes with it. His is not a space emptied of figure and story, pure and abstract; it is an innocent, dynamic space much less austere, much closer to "the dance of life." Thus he rediscovers *music*.

He shows again the sense in which architecture and dance are both ways of "visualizing music," as they were in the baroque, the classical music at once the most architectural and the most choreographic. So he rejoins something Xenakis was working on in the Philips Pavilion when he sought a "musical" way out of a static system of parallel measure.

Today one is told that abstraction can still surprise us, that its history is still before it, that it is still a live question. It is as though the *world* of abstraction had been reopened. But this means that it must be *re-thought*, breaking loose from conceptions that have long framed its discussion. Not so long ago, abstraction seemed a "dead" question, even a question of "dying"—it was supposed to play a fatal if heroic part in a drama through which painting exposed and exhausted all its formal possibilities, leaving it with no other game than an endgame. But we don't *have* to conceive of abstraction in this manner; we don't have to see it as an avant-garde post in a progressive advance to extinction. We may think of it rather as an untimely

four **Abstraction**

point in a complicated history, which goes off in several directions at once, redistributing the sense of what comes before it and what may yet come after. But for this, we need other, lighter, less mortuary ways of thinking. To rethink abstraction, we need another *kind* of theory, another picture of what it is to think "abstractly"!

In this situation, the philosophy of Gilles Deleuze becomes quite telling. Rather in the manner of fellow anti-Platonist Ludwig Wittgenstein, Deleuze advances another image of what abstraction means in philosophy, more "empiricist," more "immanentist," more "experimental"; at the same time he sketches another view of what abstraction means in art, more chaotic or formless, no longer defined in opposition to figure or image. These two kinds of abstraction intersect in many ways, forming part of a new way of doing art-connected philosophy. In both cases, we find a departure from the view of abstraction as a process of extracting pure or essential Forms, emptying a space of its concrete contents, toward another kind of abstraction and another sense of "abstract": an abstraction that consists in an impure mixing and mixing up, prior to Forms, a reassemblage that moves toward an outside rather than a purification that turns up to essential Ideas or in toward the constitutive "forms" of a medium. For Deleuze, philosophy itself becomes a practice of this abstract mixing and rearranging, a great, prodigious conceptual "And . . ." in the midst of things and histories. Thus he says that philosophy is impoverished when reduced to being merely *about* the arts, reflecting on their forms of judgment; for it has a much more vital role to play together *with* them, linking up with them in odd places, interfering and intersecting with them through "encounters" prior to settled judgments. To transform the picture of what it is to think abstractly is to transform the picture of the relations that abstract thought may have with the arts and so with abstraction in the arts. Thus Deleuze arrives at a picture of abstraction unlike the one that comes with the tragic story of this strange, self-possessed purity in the sea of kitsch, calling out to the painter-hero, obliging him to surrender until death.

Nots and Ands

The standard story of modern abstract painting rests on a particular conception, haunted by the empty canvas as Mallarmé had been by the blank page. Abstract is what is *not* figurative, not narrative, not illusionist, not literary, and so on, to the point where one arrives at a sanctifying negative theology in which "art" (or "painting") takes the place of "God" as That to which no predicate is ever adequate and can only be attained via the *via negativa*. Such things as the decline of religion and the rise of photography are commonly said to be responsible for this turn to the negative way, which would lead, through various routes, to the endpoint of the monochrome—Kasimir Malevich, Ad Reinhardt, Frank Stella's black paintings, etc. After such monochromatic emptiness, all would be parody, quotation, "irony," eclecticism—in other words, "postmodernism." Thus abstraction would bring an end to the canvas, authorizing a turn to "art" in an unspecific sense, without painting or instead of it—a turn from being (just) a painter to being an artist or "anartist" with no particular medium—which would be consummated in New York in the sixties, after abstract expressionism, with pop and minimalism.[1]

In this now-familiar drama, abstraction means stripping away of all image, figure, story, "content" to reach the empty or flat canvas. That is the root of many familiar ideas: abstraction as illusionist space from which the illusion has been removed, pure form without content;

pure, self-referential "literalness" opposed to any "decoration" or "theatricality"; a bride stripped bare. What the late Clement Greenberg called modernism is perhaps the most influential variant of this conception, connected to a story about cubism and the flattening of classical illusionist space, which Greenberg adapts from Hans Hofmann, adding, as motivation, a horrified escape from the world of kitsch toward a kind of optical puritanism, in which the eye, "abstracted" from all admixture with the other organs of the body, would itself become pure, formal, and so abstract.

Yet despite Greenberg's eye for the "quality" of the likes of Kenneth Noland and Jules Olitsky, the heroes of abstract expressionism come to seem the last heroes of this kind of abstraction, this kind of "modernism." After abstract expressionism appear various attempts to depart from the whole idea of the painter-hero who creates from nothing—from the anxiety of the blank surface or from surrender to the seduction of the virgin canvas—and, therefore, from an aesthetic erotic analyzed by Lacan around the same time. For in his seminar of 1960, Lacan defines sublimation as an attempt to recreate in an object the emptiness of the lost Thing, much as God had created the world out of nothing, *ex nihilo*. That is why the strange things we call art objects incorporate an emptiness surrounded by affects of anxiety, melancholy, mania, or mourning; it is why the fame that accrues to creators of such objects is so odd, rooted in envy.[2]

Yet it is not clear that the work that prides itself on coming after the supposed monochromatic endgame of abstraction (after modernism or formalism) really breaks with this anxious-heroic erotic, this negative theology of art, this "not." On the contrary, one can argue that postmodern art remains, as it were, haunted by the spirit of the abstract painting; it only repeats this game as farce, through quotation, parody, irony, alternating between mania and melancholia. Indeed the very idea of appropriation, and of what Jean Baudrillard called "the simulacrum" is fully impregnated by the tradition of melancholy and panicked reaction to loss or absence; in this respect it is quite unlike the idea of the simulacrum that a forgetful Baudrillard had appropriated from Deleuze, which involves not a loss but an *intensification* of the real, linked to a condition of things prior to Forms. In short, it is as though first in modernism, and then in postmodernism, the tale of abstraction were a long, sad illustration of Nietzsche's thesis linking asceticism and nihilism: that one would prefer to will nothing than not to will at all.

Of those who have written on abstraction, Deleuze is perhaps the least affected by such ascetic "nots." He remains singularly unseduced by the secrets of the "virgin" canvas—by the whole negative-theological picture of abstraction and its anxious erotic of an imperious Art approached only through negation, this virgin whose purity means death. Instead of the nots of negative theology, he prefers to see the "folds" of Neoplatonic *complicatio* as a source for abstraction. For in them he sees something that cannot possibly be made to "participate" in the purity of Forms and the sorts of abstraction that attain them. He finds another minor tradition of such abstract complication in Proust's signs, in Leibniz's "minimalist" monads, and in Spinoza's treatment of divine names, where it is linked to "the problem of expression," important for Deleuze's own view of abstraction. One finds something of Spinoza's "god or nature" in the manner Deleuze comes to formulate the problem of abstract expressionism in Jackson Pollock—as a problem of expressing something that can't *possibly* be figurative (hence can't possibly be a mere absence or lack of figuration), which can be shown only in an "ungrounded" (*effondé*) space, through a "plane of composition" rather than a "plan of organization," without beginning or ending, finality or totality. Pollock's "all-over" would be like Spinoza's infinity—a substance that just *is* the endless composition, decomposition, and recomposition of its finite modes, rather than something static that would underlie, enclose, or organize them.

Deleuze's view of the "space" of abstraction is, in short, not based on the great "not"—on the absence of figure, image, or story. Rather than absence and negation, abstraction has to do with the affirmation of "the outside" in the sense that Foucault develops from the thought of Maurice Blanchot in the sixties, explicitly contrasting it with the tradition of negative theology.[3] In effect, Foucault argues that modernism does not consist in an internalizing reversion to the medium but, on the contrary, in an opening of the medium out from itself, to the point where it becomes "beside itself." He thinks that this externalizing "madness" in modern works—this *absence d'oeuvre* opening to an "outside"—entails a certain blindness that enables a whole art of seeing.[4] Thus modernity doesn't consist in a melancholy purification of the means of representation, turning within to proclaim an enclosed autonomy; on the contrary, it is about untimely forces that announce other new outside possibilities, and so introduce a certain "heteronomy" in mediums. For Deleuze the basic question of modernity becomes how to think, how to write, how to paint such other or outside forces. Thus, in the "minority" of Kafka, the "chaosmos" of Joyce, and the *épuisements* of Beckett, he identifies an abstraction quite different from the self-purifying kind—that of those "abstract machines" that push art forms beyond and beside themselves, causing their very languages, as though possessed with the force of other things, to start stuttering "and . . . and . . . and . . .". He connects this stuttering abstract "and" not with dying or heroic self-extinction but with a strange anorganic vitality able to see in "dead" moments other new ways of proceeding. And *this* sort of vitality, this sort of abstraction, he thinks, is something of which we may *still* be capable, something still with us and before us.

So Deleuze declares the page is *never* blank, "the canvas is never empty."[5] To think in those terms is to have a mistaken idea of what it is to paint (or to write) and so of abstraction in painting (or writing). For before brush is put to canvas, there is the "avant-coup" of a long preparatory work that consists in getting rid of the ambient clichés in the studio and beyond; the canvas thus always starts off covered over with too many givens, too many probabilities, from which one must extract a singular space that allows for the chance of an "après-coup" of strange new virtualities, unpredictable or unforeseeable. This is what makes the act of painting always hysterical. To paint one must come to see the surface not so much as empty or blank but rather as intense, where "intensity" means filled with the unseen virtuality of other strange possibilities—one must become blind enough to see the surface as mixed or assembled in a particular transformable and deformable manner, rather than as just "flat." One can then see abstraction not as elimination of figure or story but rather as an invention of other spaces with original sorts of mixture or assemblage— a prodigious "and" that departs from classical illusionism and eventually even from figure/ground principles of composition. Flatness thus becomes only one possibility of the canvas among others, quite compatible with figuration. In fact Deleuze finds one sort of flattening spatialization in Francis Bacon—the use of *aplats* to make the figures appear next to, rather than within, the space the surrounds them, thus allowing the force of their strange matter-of-fact *figurality* to emerge.[6]

Another modernity, another abstraction. When in 1980, writing with Félix Guattari in the last plateau of *A Thousand Plateaus*, Deleuze asks directly the question "What ought one to call *abstract* in modern art?",[7] it thus comes after a long rethinking of the very idea of the modern and the abstract, whose logic Deleuze had set out in the 1960s—around the same time "after abstract expressionism" in New York, when it was it was thought that painting might be coming to an end. This logic (later reelaborated in terms of "abstract machines") describes rather well the unheroic, almost automatic *series* that one sees emerging in pop and in minimalism at that time in New York. To understand properly the answer Deleuze and Guattari give in *A Thousand Plateaus* to the question of what should be called "abstract" in modern art—"a line with variable direction, which traces no contour, and delimits no form"[8]—one needs some sense of this larger change in conceptual terrain. One needs to have rethought abstraction in its *logic*.

The Two Abstractions

The central frame for the notion of the abstract in the philosophical tradition has been that of a taxonomic tree of distinct classes or kinds. One abstracts as one moves up to higher levels of generality, just as one concretizes or instantiates as one moves downward toward particulars or specific instances of types. Thus the dialectic that Plato attributes to Socrates consists in the effort to track down the higher, more general Forms in the lower, more particular things that "participate" in them, by making sure that the lineages are pure or unmixed, following the divisions of the tree; ideas of both analogy or

resemblance and of force or potential (*dynamis*) would
be made to conform to this arborescent picture. Deleuze
argues that neither the transcendental idea of a priori
conditions nor the dialectical idea of a whole of contra-
dictions would in fact really break away from such
Platonism, for neither allows a sense of "abstract" that
permits one to move away altogether from general taxa,
transcendental categories, or dialectical totalities and
find things for which there exists no such "abstract"
model or type (what Deleuze terms "multiplicities" and
"singularities"). For that, one must reverse Platonism
and see Forms (and later conditions or totalities) as
belonging to an unlimited abstract space that precedes
and escapes them—a space that is "larger" than the
highest genera and has components "smaller" (or more
"minimal") than the lowest species (such, in the terms of
Duns Scotus, would be the indifference of Being and the
existence of "haeccities").

Thus Deleuze draws a picture of an abstract logical
space anterior to the divisions and up/down, high/low
movements within the great Platonic tree—a space that
includes a force or potential that constantly submits its
branches to unpredictable, even monstrous variations. In
Logique du sens, he offers a picture of such variations as
"series." A series differs from a set, a class, a type, or a
totality in remaining open to such forces of divergence
and deviation, which alter its contours and the sorts of
things to which it can be linked.[9] A series may then be
said to be composed of indistinct singularities rather
than the distinct particularities from which general
abstractions are made; and conversely a singularity is
what enters into a series rather than falling under a class
or particularizing a universal. Series are thus impure
mixtures that complicate and depart from pure lineages
of given ones, and in this respect are like the deviations

or swerves of what Lucretius called the *clinamen*. *Logique du sens* is Deleuze's attempt to show that the potential for such deviation and ramification forms an uneliminable anonymous layer of meaning, prior to sense, reference, and elocution. *Différence et répétition* then attempts to show that when "difference" is freed from making "distinctions" or "oppositions" within or among the fixed classes of the tree, it discovers a complex sort of repetition—a whole complicated time and movement that includes a nonprobabilistic "nomadic" kind of chance, which no throw of categorical dice can ever abolish.

One might then say that there are two sorts of abstraction in Deleuze, two senses of what it is to abstract and to be abstract. The first is the Platonic sense of abstract Form. It is the object of the "critique of abstractions" that Henri Bergson shared with his contemporary William James, and that Deleuze himself formulates when, saying that he is an empiricist in the tradition of Alfred North Whitehead, he declares, "The abstract does not explain, but must itself be explained."[10] To explain *by* abstractions is to start with abstract Forms and ask how they are realized in the world or extracted from it. But to explain those abstractions themselves is to reinsert them in a larger (and smaller) "pluralistic" world that includes multiplicities that subsist in Forms and induce variations in them, altering their connections with other things. In this way one shows *that* they are abstract in the invidious sense of being incapable of complication or movement—such is the critique. Thus one attains a complicated condition in things prior to Forms, which Deleuze likens to the space traced by one of Pollock's lines, which "does not go from one point to another, but passes between the points, ceaselessly bifurcating and diverging."[11] One arrives at another question: not how are Forms are extracted from or realized in things, but under what conditions can something new or singular be produced "outside" them? Thus one comes to the second sense of the abstract in Deleuze, developed along with Guattari through the concept of abstract machines and "opposed to abstract in the ordinary sense"[12]—the sense of the "and" that moves outside. To pass from the first critical sense of the abstract to this second, "affirmative" one is to transform the very idea of the *abs-tractus*—the act of withdrawal or turning away.

For as long as one thinks of the *abs-tractus* as Form withdrawn from matter, one thinks in terms of possibilities and their realizations (or later transcendental or dialectical conditions of such possibility). The basic assumption remains that the world is logically congruent with possibilities given by abstractions, even if all such possibilities are not realized or instantiated or if all categories under which they fall are not known. But once one allows for a world that is disunified, incongruous, composed of multiple divergent paths, one can think in terms of abstract virtualities that, in contrast to such abstract possibilities, are quite real, even though they are not actualized. One starts to see the force or potential of things for which there exists no abstract concept, since their effectuation would go off in too many directions or "senses" at once. Deleuze calls such *potentia* "virtual" in a sense that contrasts with the "possible" developed by Bergson in his critique of abstractions.[13] Thus the virtual may be said to be "abstract" in a different sense from the possible: unlike abstract "mechanisms," abstract machines are said to be "real although not concrete, actual although not effectuated,"[14] comprising a sort of "real virtuality" in things. They have the abstraction of immanent force rather than transcendental form—the abstract virtuality within things of other different things, of other "possible worlds" in our world, other histories in our history. That is why they are "rhizomatic" rather than "arborescent"—serial, differential, complicating rather than categorical, generalizing and purifying. That is why they can be expressed only through abstract "diagram" and not abstract "code." The whole problem is how to put them first, how to *see* them as first, for the two sorts of abstraction do not exist apart from one another. They are inseparable forces at work and at odds within any logical space, including that of Plato himself (for example, in the aporia of the "bastard logic" of the *chora* in the *Timaeus*). In the reversal of Platonism one is thus put first, reversing what it means to come first or be prior (priority of immanent condition rather than of transcendental form). That is why the passage from one kind of abstraction to the other involves a change in seeing: rather than seeing the Forms that the sun illuminates above, or the ideas that the natural light illuminates within, one must learn to see this prior, immanent condition that illuminates through multiple paths outside, "ceaselessly bifurcating and diverging," like one of Pollock's lines.

Deleuze then brings this second sense of "abstract" to his discussion of modern art—for example, to Jean-Luc Godard. For if Deleuze sees Godard films as abstract, it is not because they remove all narrative or *diegesis* and retreat into pure filmic self-reference but because they take singular elements from all over, past and present, and reassemble them, mixing them up in the strange nonnarrative continuity of an "abstract machine."[15] The motivation is thus not the removal or absence of narrative but an attempt to attain an outside of other odd connections through a free, abstract "and," which takes over the movement and time of the film. That is one source of Deleuze's quarrel with the film semiology of Christian Metz. One must put this sort of abstraction first, see it as first, and so take narration as only "an indirect consequence that flows from movement and time, rather than the other way around."[16] For film is not a code of which abstraction would be the self-reference; it is an abstract machine that has movement and time as specific abstract virtualities, which then get effectuated in particular social and political conditions; narrative is only one restricted possibility of film. Thus what Deleuze counts as most specific to film—the forces of its time and movement images—is at the same time what opens original connections with other mediums, for example, with architecture, which Deleuze then sees as closer to film than is theater.

But it is the same with abstraction in painting. There too we find an abstraction of the "and" rather than of the "is," of the outside rather than of the absence of figuration and narration; and there too the problem is to see such abstraction as first. Much as with Metz in film theory, in painting theory one might thus draw a contrast with Clement Greenberg's attempt to see in abstraction an apotheosis of autonomy and "opticality." For following Lessing's classical division of the arts, Greenberg argues, in effect, that abstraction in each art form (for which abstract painting takes the lead and shows the way) would achieve an absolute separation where each would stay in its place and appeal to one and only one sense organ; thus the "eye" of painting would at last be freed from all theatricality, and be shown only what is purely optical. Greenberg's contrast is with the Wagnerian *Gesamtkunstwerk*, which tries to put all arts and senses together in a totality. Deleuze is concerned to undercut the logic of this contrast, which opposes clear, distinct elements to total expressive forms. In his own logic, he allows for things to be inseparably connected while remaining singular and nontotalized and so remains undisturbed by "paradoxical" objects that fall in between the supposed bounds of specific mediums, mixing them up anew; and he thus envisages other, lighter Nietzschean paths out of Wagnerian totality.[17]

Pollock's Lines

As narrative in film depends on the abstract virtualities of movement and time, so figuration or image in painting may be said to depend on how pictorial space is held together and comes apart—on how it achieves an order out of chaos. There are different kinds of abstraction and different types of "figurability" in painting, and these differences are more important to its logic than the gross opposition between the abstract and the representational. Deleuze then tries to spell out this "logic of sensation" in painting.

One can think of pictorial space as built up from distinct simple elements or else as held together by expressive wholes or by figure/ground gestalts. But Deleuze's logic envisages another complicating possibility, prior to these or subsisting within them: he thinks that pictorial space can become ungrounded (*effondé*) and "disparated" in its composition, allowing for the force of indistinctions, in-between spaces, or "leakages" (*fuites*). In this case, pictorial space attains an uncentered, unbounded, and formless condition; it discovers the workings of nonprobabilistic chance in its composition; and it departs from the predominance of purely *optisch* frontal vision to discover more *haptisch* sorts of spatialization, which have multiple entrances and exits rather than being given to a single point of view. Thus Deleuze proposes to distinguish fixed visual plans of organization in delimited spaces from free, tactile planes of disparate distribution in unlimited or formless ones. What he finds important about Pollock's abstract line is a passage from one to the other, or a reversal in which one is put first; he sees a turn from the centered, framed, figure/ground organization that European classicism took to be universal, to another uncentered, unlimited, *informel*, multiple sort of distribution in space and space of distribution. He says that Greenberg is quite right in pointing to the importance of the abandonment of the easel in this shift, for it is what made possible a "reversion" in pictorial space from "visual horizon" to "tactile ground."[18] But to give up the easel is more than to abandon the figurative or illusionistic relation to nature. It is to depart as well from delimitation (frames or borders), perspectival distance, and presumptions of symmetry or of organic centering; and it is therefore very odd of Greenberg to say that these changes result in a pure "opticality." For what in fact is at stake is the discovery of something *prior* to the contoured or delimited figure—something "first," which comes "before" the horizons of frontal vision and cannot simply be derived from a purification or flattening of the classical *optisch* perspective space. What Pollock discovers, according to Deleuze, is rather the "catastrophe" of the visual—catastrophe not as a content (as in romanticism) but as a force or potential inherent in pictorial space as such. For all painting passes through an experience of "the collapse of visual coordinates," as a condition bringing other singular visual sensations into being; such is the "blindness" that lets a painter see and show the things unseen before him. Remarking on how such catastrophe figures in Cézanne and Klee, Deleuze declares that painting is the art form closest to it. Thus he calls painting inherently hysterical in his study of Francis Bacon, where the catastrophe appears in the operational cluster of "asignifying" features, *taches*, zones, which Bacon terms the "diagram" in his works.

Because Pollock's line thus has variable direction, tracing no contour and delimiting no form, ceaselessly diverging and bifurcating, it requires a rethinking of the very idea of the abstract. Greenberg's story based in cubism, and the sort of three-dimensional space that allows one to see depths and contours, figures and grounds, is not sufficient. For just what matters in Pollock's abstraction are lines and *taches* of color that don't limit anything, that have no inside or outside, no convexity or concavity—and so are after all "Gothic" in a sense that Deleuze finds in the writings of Wilhelm Worringer rather than in surrealism. For this abstraction departs from geometric, rectilinear shape; it is less a spiritual purification of Form than an expressive decomposition of matter. It is thus "abstract" in a peculiar sense, which makes Mondrian's squares or Kandinsky's points, lines, and planes still seem strangely figurative, since they after all remain "figures" with delimited contours.

Indeed it is as though such earlier rectilinear kinds of abstraction were an attempt to reduce the forces of abstract diagram in painting, so as to attain the purity of an abstract code of primitive visual elements—a sort of spiritualizing escape from the potential catastrophe of the visual toward a fundamental language of the organization of color, form, and shape. Pollock then helps restore the diagram to abstraction, allowing one retrospectively to see a prefigurative, formless materialism already at work in the geometries of the earlier abstract work. Thus Deleuze detects "nomadic contourless" lines in Kandinsky, while the unequal thickness of the sides of Mondrian's squares suggests the possibility of a contourless diagonal. Deleuze's student Bernard Cache has gone on to try to see such possibilities in the baroque "inflections" of Klee's pedagogical sketchbooks, as well as in a strange Lucretian materialism that would precede

Kandinsky's official rectilinear spiritualism. In both cases
Cache finds an abstract space composed through inflec-
tion, vector, and frame rather than organized by point,
line, and plane.[19] At the same time the contourless,
unlimited abstract space that Pollock attains changes the
terms of the contrast between the abstract and the figurative. It helps us see other relations to figure, other
kinds of "figurality," like that Deleuze finds in Bacon.
Thus Deleuze says that Bacon departs from images-
given-in-classical-perspectival-distance in yet another
way, different from the abstractions of either Kandinsky
or Pollock—from a cliché-ridden "photographic" world
he extracts an original kind of figure placed on a strange,
intolerable surface from which it is always seeking
release, as though subjected to the violence of invisible
forces that undo its "faciality" and expose its "meat."

In *A Thousand Plateaus* Deleuze and Guattari thus
declare that the emergence of the abstract line "with
variable direction, that traces no contour, and delimits
no form" requires that what counts as abstract be itself
rethought along several lines at once. First, the gross
exclusive opposition between figurative and abstract
looses its centrality, and a good deal of its interest, in
favor of kinds of pictorial space and the kinds of figurability they permit. For images or figures are not
created out of nothing to match external models; they
come into being from a compositional space that
always departs from visual coordinates, creating
strange new sensations. Abstraction is thus not in the
first instance to be understood as the emptying of illusionist space of figures and stories; it is rather a "sensation" of this other larger abstract space that precedes
and exceeds them. "Figuration" is a limiting case of the
original abstract potential for "figurability" in painting.
This, however, requires a change in the presumed

motivation of abstraction: not to strip everything away in self-referential abnegation, but to offer sensations of things that can be seen only through the experience of "the collapse of the visual" or the "blindness" of painting. In that sense, *what* one paints is always otherwise unseeable abstract *forces*. Finally, the "space" of abstraction is not originally or fundamentally geometric—"the abstract line is not in the first instance rectilinear."[20] Geometric form looses its centrality in favor of more tactile, dispersed, uncentered, and unlimited sorts of space. Thus Deleuze and Guattari suggest that we think of the classical Athenian preoccupation with geometric or rectilinear form as only one possibility, preceded, according to Riegl, by an Egyptian one, and followed, according to Worringer, by a Gothic one; one can then see the classical space of perspectival distance in terms of the *optisch/haptisch* distinction rather than in simple terms of form and content. Yet there remains an idealism in the *Kunstwollen* offered by Riegl or Worringer, linked to the preoccupations of a German Eurocentrism. For in fact painting *starts* as abstract and is such already in prehistoric times. Thus Deleuze and Guattari draw attention to the argument advanced by André Leroi-Gourhan that "art is abstract from the outset and could not be otherwise at its origin."[21] Classical European illusionism is thus only a late development in an inherently abstract art. For all of these reasons, Deleuze and Guattari say that, far from resulting from stripping illusionist space bare, abstraction is something prior to it—something that comes first. It is first historically, as Leroi-Gourhan shows; it is first in motivation, since all painting passes through a prefigurative or preformal "blindness"; and it is first logically, since the classical distanced, centered way of showing contours and forms is only a lim-

ited case of the larger potential in painting of a center-
less, contourless, boundless, formless space.[22]

The World of Abstraction

What is then abstract? Today the question arises in relation to what is known as the "information" age. Perhaps
some new pragmatist will apply the critique of abstractions found in Bergson and James to the very idea of
information and the computational paradigm to which it
belongs. Two related postulates might be distinguished.
The first says that information is independent of the
material medium through which it is transmitted; the
second says that simulation and reality come to the same
thing. Thus one "abstracts" from material support and,
by replicating processes, abstracts them from the particularities of their real existence; even "life" becomes only
abstract information, which can be replicated and so
made artificially. The two postulates of immateriality and
irreality then combine in the great conceit of the info
era: that electronic devices will abolish real or material
space and time and transport us all into another abstract,
bodiless "space" or "reality," consummating the triumph
of silicon over carbon.

By contrast in Deleuze one finds an abstraction concerned not with extracting information from things (as
though the material world were so much clumsy hard-
ware) but rather with finding within things the delicate,
complicated abstract virtualities of other things. Such
abstraction doesn't entail independence or transferability
from material support and doesn't operate according to a
logic of simulation. Rather inherent in materials it supposes the subsistence of connections that exceed the
messages of a medium and ourselves as senders and
receivers of them. Thus the abstract use of a medium is
not when it itself becomes the message, but when it

starts to stammer "and . . . and . . . and . . ." prior to message and transmission. In this way, abstraction belongs to the bodily material world and its unpredictable chaosmotic processes—processes so formless as to permit the operations of abstract machines with which computational devices may be then themselves be connected. Thus Deleuze has little sympathy for the reductive proposition, dear to computational neuroscience, that the mind just *is* the information program of the brain. To the Cartesian "ghost in the machine" that Gilbert Ryle ridiculed, Deleuze prefers what Spinoza called "the spiritual automaton"—this finite manner of being that composes and recomposes with others in an unlimited field, ever connecting and reconnecting the mind *and* the body through a whole "technology of the self." If then the brain is a connection device, it is not mind-programmed but plunged in a multiple, disunified, formless world. Its logic is therefore not the purely computational one of which Alan Turing dreamed, but operates instead with form and formlessness, order and chaos, rather like what Deleuze finds in abstract painting and Pollock's line. The question of abstraction then becomes: To what sort of abstract machines do Turing machines belong, and with what sort of "desiring machines" are they connected?

One can then imagine other links to the space of abstract painting than the one proposed by neogeo (where "geo" simulates the irreality of "info") or than attempts such as Mark Johnson's to redescribe Kandinsky's abstract spiritual code in a language of cognitive psychology.[23] Rather Deleuze is drawn to models in science and mathematics that come with strong software capabilities, that depart from distinct sets and expressive totalities to envisage things like catastrophe, chaos, and complexity. They can be used to generate topographical spaces more like Pollock than

Kandinsky—nongeometric or nonrectilinear, prior to the "simulation" of things. Info devices don't *have* to be used to assist smart weapons or to imagine what it was like to walk about in the Egyptian pyramids. There are other "abstract" uses.

The situation of our postindustrial info devices today is thus something like that in which Deleuze sees the new "industrial art" of cinema at the turn of the century, when Bergson proposed his own critique of abstractions. Bergson feared a "cinematographic illusion" of continuity, but already the real problem of cinema was not that of image and reality any more than of medium and message (or medium *being* the message). It was a problem of time and movement in the composition of space, and so of other, more diverging and bifurcating conceptions of continuity, taken up in Bergson's own philosophy. And it was just when cinema made such "abstract" connections in its new industrial "material" that it discovered its most intense relations with abstraction in the other materials, in architecture and dance as well as painting and sculpture.[24] Such were then the abstract virtualities in the medium, irreducible to messages, which unfolded within particular sociopolitical situations, punctuated by the experience of the war; such were the abstract forces in the medium that would figure in larger abstract machines, connected to an outside, exposing things unthought in our ways of being, seeing, and doing.

Perhaps the most intense relation our current info machines might have with abstraction in painting—old, new, yet to come—is of this sort. For the relation between mediums (and abstraction in mediums) is one not of negation but of connection—of "and" rather than "not." A new medium with its specific materiality never simply takes over the functions of older ones, as though abstract information were being transferred from one means of delivery to another—photography depriving painting of its functions, video images killing off film images, everything being replaced by interactivity. Thus, for his part, Deleuze refuses to join certain influential directors or critics in making video responsible for the decline of the "abstract" cinema that came after the war with Italian neorealism, French new wave, and American experimental film. He thinks the problem is more general. What is at stake is a loss of the taste for the *world* given through the odd descriptive space that such "abstract" film opened up—a loss of the sense of the world, shown in philosophy at the same time by a retreat from conceptual movement into a meta-reflection on abstract norms of communication, in a replay of the neo-Kantian denunciation of Bergson by Julien Benda.[25]

For this *world* is what abstraction is all about: abstraction as the attempt to show—in thought as in art, in sensation as in concept—the odd, multiple, unpredictable potential in the midst of things of other new things, other new mixtures.[26]

five **Grounds**

"Ground" is a word like "foundation," with uses in both philosophy and architecture suggesting some deep analogy or affinity between the two.[1] More modestly, the word may be said to have a conceptual potential that one can exploit to suggest new ways of thinking and perhaps also of building. That is what I propose to do. I will take "ground" as a nodal or synaptic word in a complex mixing different architectural and philosophical senses, which I will try to unfold.

A classical source for this exercise may be found in Heinrich Wölfflin's *Prolegomena to a Psychology of Architecture* (1886)—a sort of philosophical manifesto of what it means to build in a milieu.[2] Wölfflin combines Kant's idea of the schematism and of the architectonic whole with Schopenhauer's notion that architecture is the art of overcoming heaviness or gravity and the resistance of matter. Thus for Wölfflin, the ground has to do with a basic *Formlosigkeit* (formlessness) that the will, as a vital force immanent in things, must overcome; the *Formkraft* (force of form) is to pull us up from this formless state, against which all of life struggles. The principles of regularity, symmetry, proportion, and harmony all derive from this idea. Heaviness or gravity is thus a vital matter. It appears when breathing gets slow, its rhythm irregular, as in the state of melancholia that Wölfflin sees in a painting by Dürer of that title, which depicts a woman staring mournfully at an irregular and unmeasurable stone block that, as Wölfflin points out, appears to be falling down toward the ground. But painting is not the primary art of formlessness and vital grounding; it is rather architecture, the *Baukunst* or set of tectonic arts, and Wölfflin expresses astonishment that there is no philosophy of it.

But let me now jump to some points in modern architecture and thought, where the question of grounds and forms has been raised in ways that are still part of our history. I'll start with a very familiar case, that of Le

Corbusier, though similar things may be said about glass and "dematerialization" in Mies. Let's take for example what Le Corbusier says about "artificial sites" in 1933 in *The Radiant City*. There he dismisses the "natural ground" as a "dispenser of rheumatism and tuberculosis" and declares the natural site to be the "enemy of man."[3] Thus we should sever the traditional connection between building and ground, giving up the sort of continuity where a building is the figure whose ground is supplied by its natural setting. With such "artificiality" goes a kind of abstraction. The house becomes an "abstraction" of vertical and horizontal planes, the floor plan free to take on various configurations and the facade open for various kinds of transparency. As with the Maison Dom-ino, the house is thus freed from the earth of historical tradition to move in an extendable boundless space, acquiring a Mondrian-like autonomy, where the ground is only a vestige. Take the illustration that Le Corbusier captions "The architectural revolution is complete." The before picture shows load-bearing masonry walls sunk deep into the earth, holding up poorly lit little box rooms; the after picture, against a neutral light background, shows a rectilinear structure, opened up, with a feel of airy impermanence, raised off the ground to allow a car underneath. In this revolution, houses will be put on *pilotis* barely touching the ground, roofs flattened, and everything turned into intersecting horizontal and vertical planes and monochromatic stucco surfaces. That is what we can do once we see the ground as a source of false naturalism. "Ungrounded" thus acquires the sense of "off-the ground," freed from the "weight" of tradition, artificial rather than natural, abstract rather than figurative—abstract in a now canonical sense of reduction to a pure or universal language, reproducible anywhere, irrespective of the natural site.

A series of oppositions would grow up surrounding this idea of ground—the natural vs. the artificial, the organic vs. the abstract, the figural vs. the geometric, the contextual vs. the autonomous—the architectural revolution being the act that replaces the first set of terms with the "new order" of the second. There would be many reactions. Some would try to revalorize the first pole of these oppositions—the natural, the organic, the figural, the contextual, the "site-specific." I would like to look instead at several attempts to get out from under these oppositions themselves, finding other spaces lying in between them—in other words, to unground *them*. While my cases are quite different from one another, they all share three features concerning the question of ground. First is the attempt to move away from "proper" visual form, geometric or rectilinear, horizontal and vertical; thus "ungrounded" no longer means off-the-ground but rather has to do with a kind of form-giving movement prior to the ground as understood in autonomous up-down structures. Thus, secondly, there emerges a sense of "ungrounded" not as a state to be achieved once and for all, as in a revolution completed, but rather as a potential or force in things that must be shown or released. In the third place, we then find notions of history or memory that move away from the progressive time of a "new order" toward a more complicated sense of time as a process, always unfinished, to be taken up again in unforeseeable circumstances, as though each period brought with it a potential ungrounding that architecture might exploit, release, or show.

My first case is Peter Eisenman. I think that in several senses his early houses may be said still to move within the series of modernist oppositions I associated with Le Corbusier, with their sense of autonomy, rectilinearity, and artificiality. The question of "grounds" is raised in the rethinking that comes with his turn to "cities of artificial excavation," which return to the question of how buildings are "grounded" in their urban sites and therefore "ungrounded" or released from them. But Eisenman refuses to go back to figure/ground relations or continuities. For he here conceives the urban setting as an accumulation of superimposed layers in which the partially invisible "memory" of cities is deposited. What matters is thus a "geology" of urban memory in which one can move about through superposition, juxtaposition, grafting. From this there arises a sense of space more Piranesian than Mondrianesque, in which figures are freed to move against the fundamentally ungrounded mnemonic geology of the site. There follows a shift in the sense of artifice. Eisenman's "artificial cities" are artificial in a sense different from that of Le Corbusier's "artificial sites." Artifice is no longer opposed to the natural site but instead becomes a kind of fiction that intervenes with respect to the joints or connections that supply urban memory with its false or "natural" sense of continuity. Thus superpositions and odd connections among different strata of time can be established much as in cinema montage. Armed with this idea of the artifice of fiction as a power prior to narrative continuities and sure judgments, Eisenman moves away from the "progressivism" of the idea of a completable architectural revolution. Instead one finds something akin to Borges's idea of the labyrinth, as in his fable of the garden of ever-forking paths. It is as though there were no period in history that did not contain points of divergence that open onto other histories, such that the "joints" of time can become undone at certain moments and things can go "out of joint."[4] What emerges from Eisenman's "stratigraphic" conception of urban memory is thus a "disjointed" architectural style that seeks a plane, at once historical and formal, prior to the opposition between modernist abstraction and post-modernist contextualism.

No doubt there is much to be said about this outlook and the directions in which it would take Peter, but there were also other attempts to rethink the idea of ground. For example, some people were impressed by the architectural "cuts" that Gordon Matta-Clark incised in derelict settings. Here ungrounding as a process goes together with unbuilding or undoing, providing another route out of contextualism. Thus Dan Graham would see in Matta-Clark's interventions an antimonumentalism that contrasts with the attempt to retrieve the context of the historical city through architectural form.[5] For they exposed not an architectural memory in monuments but a subversive memory hidden by social and architectural facades with their false sense of integrity or wholeness, breaking out through the openings in the body of banal spaces. Today some critics have gone back to Matta-Clark, seeing in his work a continuation of a theme in Robert Smithson, according to which the Earth is no longer conceived as a stable ground but rather as an entropic force ever undoing the "information" of formal structures; yet it remains an open question how such "unbuilding" might move from such para-architectural activities to become a part of building itself.[6]

There has been another alternative, which introduces an ungrounding that derives neither from artificial excavation nor from antimonumental intervention but rather from a sort of "dynamic topology." Such topologies attempt to move away from the classical relation between gravity and vision, weight and upright posture, through which Wölfflin, for example, rediscovered the sense of proportion and harmony, the *concinnitas* of

Alberti and Vitruvius. "Formlessness" now becomes a positive feature of visual space, even of an anorganic vitality. For example, the faceless figures in the paintings of Francis Bacon reveal an undoing of the Albertian relations between face and ground in favor of another kind of corporeal space, shown as well in the loss of the skeleton/flesh relation, flesh becoming "meat"—soft, malleable, perhaps even bloblike.[7]

Today of course we have many examples of architecture proud to depart from Corbusian right angles along some such topological lines; soon we may even see them lumped together as a new style. For my third case, I will take someone not likely to be included in this group, who came to architecture from painting back in the 1950s to work in Paris with the Groupe Espace. This group was quite opposed to right angles, admiring in Le Corbusier something one rather sees in Ronchamp or the Philips Pavilion. I am referring to Paul Virilio, who is better known for his writings on electronic technologies, which in fact came to the fore with his break with Claude Parent and the Groupe Espace. I'll say something about that in a minute.

The Groupe Espace still spoke in the tone of a manifesto: "We are now confronted by the overriding necessity to accept as a historical fact the end of the vertical axis of elevation, and the end of the horizontal as permanent plane, in order to defer to the oblique axis and the inclined plane, which realize all the necessary conditions of the creation of a new urban order and permit as well a total reinvention of the architectural vocabulary. This tipping of the plane must be understood for what it is: the third spatial possibility of architecture."[8] There had been a horizontality of villages and landed populations, then a verticality of metropolises and skyscrapers. Above all the Groupe Espace detested tall towers. The "oblique function" promised a new idea: a topological conception of urban spaces linked to movements made possible through "oriented surfaces that allow the ground to be covered." As against modern verticality, the oblique function would allow for what Virilio would call a "reeroticization of the ground" as a sort of folded or pleated force field.[9] Virilio had come under the influence of Maurice Merleau-Ponty at the time. His idea of a new "ground" for architectural space was to be part of a more general rediscovery of the body or "the flesh"—part of a more general phenomenological critique of the abstract Cartesian space that was supposed to have led "European science" into a state of crisis. Virilio was drawn to Gestalt theory and the attempt to derive figure/ground relations from upright posture and frontal vision, thus rediscovering a topic central to Wölfflin—the relations between ground and form, gravity and vision.

But for Virilio the events of '68 in Paris meant a break with this group and its project or manifesto. As he puts it: "I dropped the issue of space completely to focus on topics like time, speed, dromology . . . time and politics."[10] Instead of a new urban order with more grounded spatial possibilities for architecture, he saw the emergence and global spread of an ungrounded media civilization, eventually moving in real-time transmission, which abolished the phenomenological sense of groundedness, proximity, and gravity or at least introduced a new sense of "dislocation" into it. Thus there is a certain tension in his thought between a grounded lived space and an ungrounded "live" time; and Virilio diagnoses many maladies that the body would suffer when deprived by the new electronic time-space of its properly grounded sense of distance and proximity. It is as though the body, which used to be nicely grounded in the per-

spectival space of the classical European city, were to suffer from a generalized disorientation in the global cities
of our information societies: an inertia, a panic, a hyper-
activity, even a screen addiction. This side of Virilio's
thought seems consistent with a critical phenomenological view of the body in the age of smart machines, as for
example with the complaint that with computer-assisted
design goes a loss of the "bodily feel" of architectural or
urban space given through drawing.

But another line in Virilio's thought seems to depart
from the traditional phenomenological view of a corpo-
really grounded lived space, in which the Earth doesn't
move and in which the body is thought to be "situated"
or "thrown into the world," and hence from the senses of
grounding that Heidegger would associate with the identity or "being there" of historical peoples. Instead it
works with a dynamic view of the body, according to
which movement or *trajets* constitute our corporeal space
and make us who are. This view leads to an eroticization
not of the ground but of dynamic process of ungrounding, indeed eroticization *as* an ungrounding or release of
the ungrounded movements of the sort seen in Klee's
pedagogical notebooks or in Kleist's fine essay on puppet
theater. Ungrounded movement is then the movement
that is no longer bound to move from one fixed point to
another but rather traces its own unbounded space
through the trajectories or paths that it takes.

Virilio expresses this dynamic view of our bodily
being when he says that we are constituted by a corporeal "trajectivity" prior to our subjectivity and objectivity.
In these terms we might think about the "desituating"
features of the new electronic spaces—for example, our
ability to move about in them unseen and unnamed—as
something other than a phenomenological nightmare.
We might use it to envisage in new ways the "becoming

city" of our bodies, the "becoming body" of our cities, and the spaces in which such becomings transpire. For much as it is said that axonometric drawing disposes us to an overly rectilinear or segmented view of the possibilities of architectural space that a dynamic topology might correct, so one might say that the concept of "program" may dispose us to an overly operational view of the space through which our bodies acquire their trajectivity, which another less programmatic, more affective diagram might allow us to see. A new question then arises: What kinds of spaces or constructions might accommodate, show, facilitate, release, these ungrounded sorts of movement, encounter, connection, for example in urban spaces, and the ways in which we fill them out? What would an architecture of such trajectories and movements look like, and what larger philosophy of the body might it suppose?

Such a philosophy would require, I think, a sense of indetermination in the conception of who we are, and so in the movements that our bodies make in the space of our lives. We must see ourselves as vague or indefinite beings prior to the fixed qualities that tie us to grounds or lands, and so as beings always able to be released from such qualities. For there are always points in our lives where we may move away from such grounds or identities on a kind of uncharted voyage, which form part of the multiple geographies and landscapes that make us who we are as corporeal beings. As indeterminate spatial bodies, we are thus something else than calculating individuals, organic members of communities, or even cheerful participants in a nice "civil society." We have other "powers," which raise other sorts of questions concerning our social being: those of the times and spaces through which the singularities that make our lives indefinite might freely intersect, connect, assemble.

Perhaps then we need to get away from the picture that social life has roots in the ground or soil that supplies it with its basic sense and circumscribes the movements of which it is capable—that the life-world is in the first instance a grounded world. We find this picture in the great divisions that the sociology of the last century associated with the emergence of the nation-state— the divisions between modernity and tradition, individual and community. Thus one was said to be "grounded" in tradition or community, "ungrounded" in modernity or as an individual. One was offered the unattractive alternative of being either an individual atom moving about in a Cartesian social space or an integral member of an organic whole, fitting together in an Aristotelian social place. A quite different picture derives from views that combine the sense of indetermination with another notion of the spaces of social movement and therefore of the social whole.[11] They introduce another view of modernity than the one that divides us up into "possessive" individuals and "nurturing" communities. Modernity is not the process that passes from the first to the second, from community to contract. It is a process that constantly turns us into indeterminate beings who fit neither into communities with their collective narratives nor into the "self-organizing systems" of acquisitive individuals with their more or less rational interactions—beings who thus become "ungrounded" and so don't integrate quite so easily into the modern nation-state. There is a simple reason why. The modern world unleashes patterns of demography or migration that put people in situations where, in relation to themselves and to one another, they are no longer able to tell straight narratives of their "origins." They become originals without origins; their narratives become ungrounded, out of joint, constructed by superposition or juxtaposition rather than by development or progress; a "time" of socially ungrounded movement is thus introduced into their being. The "transnational" situation of both corporations and immigrations that Saskia Sassen finds in our global cities, along with the new divisions they introduce and the new "movements" they may yet invent, is a contemporary case in point.[12]

In such a conception of social space, we can all be said to be potential "anybodies" before being turned into "somebodies." There is thus an indefiniteness in the "life" of the body, which may be associated with the word *anybody*, and contrasted with the particularities that delimit us as definite somebodies determined or grounded in space and time. One might speak of a principle of the indefiniteness of the body: each of us has *a* body in this indefinite sense, each of us is *an* anybody or is capable of becoming anybody. The indefiniteness of corporeal being is thus impersonal yet quite singular: to have *a* body, to be able to become anybody, is in fact what is most *peculiar* to each of us, even though it never reduces to anything particular about us, since it supposes that there is always something yet "to be constructed" in our bodily being and being together.[13] There is no one who is not possessed of such a singular, indefinite body, *closer* to us than "our bodies, ourselves"—than our *particular* bodies and selves, our *communal* bodies and selves. The potential of our indefinite yet singular bodily being means that we are "close to" and "distant from" ourselves and one another in peculiar, unplannable ways. Once we give up the belief that our life-world is rooted in the ground, we may thus come to a point where ungroundedness is no longer experienced as existential anxiety and despair but as a freedom and a lightness that finally allow us to *move*.

Movement and indetermination belong together; neither can be understood without the other.

To come back to the young Heinrich Wölfflin, twenty-two years old, astonished in his thesis that philosophy had no principles for the "schematism" of the body in architecture, nor therefore for the corporeal sources of the spiritual. We might imagine someone taking up this question again today but without the assurances of the Kantian architectonic or of the a priori nature of the schematism. Then we would have not only a different "psychology of architecture," working with another kind of relation between grounds and forms, but also a different style of thought, working with another sense of bodily schemata and history. Thus I come to perhaps the most critical point in this exercise. It is a matter of priorities, of what one puts first. Must we conceive of ungrounding in terms of fixed or determinate grounds, indefinite anybodies in terms of situated or localized somebodies? Or can we put ungrounding first, analyzing the relations between grounds and forms, grounds and identities, in terms of the potential for free ungrounded movement that is always virtual in them?

Today,
armed with com-
puters, architects want
to depart from the orthogonal and the rectilinear—it
has already become something
of a fashion. But what does this
voyage outside the orthogonal in fact
allow us to do; how does it affect us?
It seems appro-
priate to ask this
question about Peter Eisenman and on the occasion   *six*   **Other Geometries**
of the opening of the Aronoff Center. For the sinu-
ous, skew geometries of the connective tissue of this
work apparently introduce a sort of "affective space"
of unanticipated encounter and connection, letting people
see and be seen from odd angles, creating momentary little worlds: that is
one "operation." It probably would not have been possible using nice
Corbusian right angles or within the larger aegis of the *concinnitas* of
Albertian space; it shows that great classical convention to be
strangely constricting or limiting. Geometry is thus something
more than a simple decoration or sculptural form given to a
calm external eye; forms are used for other aims, to affect us
in other ways. That in any case is the ambition. For it
has long been the desire of this architect to challenge the assumptions, the conventions,
the typologies of architecture;
and this work is

no exception. Our question may then be put in this way: How can "other geometries" help change the very sense of "constructible space" and so of what architecture may yet do? I will try to get at this question and this ambition through a brief excursion into some related philosophical problems about form and geometry, which might in turn take us back to architecture and this architect.

The Other
What then is the problem of "other geometries"— "geometry" in what sense and other to what? We can talk, for example, of the geometry of a novel or a character in a novel, or else of another person, someone in fear or in pain, with a toothache. Such are the geometries of living—the geometry of a young Japanese woman walking down a Parisian street or a Dutchman made to feel clumsy, elephantine, in a traditional Japanese house or inn. Each of us has such geometries, composed of lines of different kinds, coming to us in various ways, which make up the arrangements or dispositions of space—the "assemblages"—in which we move and relate to one another. But how then do such geometries of living come together, intersecting and interfering with one another in the space of a city or a building?

We might distinguish between two kinds of spatial disposition, effective and affective. In the first, one tries to insert movements, figures, stories, activities into some larger organization that predates and survives them; the second, by contrast, seeks to release figures or movements from any such organization, allowing them to go off on unexpected paths or relate to one another in undetermined ways. We can already see that "construction" and "intuition" acquire different senses in the two cases. The first tries to draw all the lines of our various geometries from the fixed points of a prior system, while the second works through a more informal diagram that throws together odd features in a loose intuition that creates its own points as it goes along; and we may thus speak of two kinds of "geometry." Yet the distinction remains a conceptual one, for there is perhaps no building or city space in which both kinds of geometry don't exist at once, at least potentially. Any constructed space always reveals a tension between the two, the question being which one we put first. Thus, for example, even in pictures or buildings made from classical Albertian perspective, other things in fact go on according to the principle "God exists, therefore everything is permitted."

Once we think of the "geometries of living" along such lines, we encounter a first philosophical problem. It is a classical problem—the problem of the other, of *autrui*. The late Gilles Deleuze formulates it in an original way, connected to our question of geometry: he says that the other is the "expression of a possible world" that doesn't exist outside the expression—that of a frightened face, for example.[1] The problem is then one of the body, its modes of spatialization and expression. Writing and painting help see it as if engaged in a kind of "spatial investigation" proceeding by experiment and induction. For example, Michel Tournier uses fiction to ask what would happen to our "geometries of living" should we find ourselves without *autrui* as a condition of our experience—if we were thus quite alone without the assemblages of either cities or buildings.[2]

Jean-Paul Sartre, playwright and philosopher, formulates the problem of *autrui* in another way: "Hell is other people." But Deleuze finds that the Sartrian problematic of the gaze in fact restores the traditional subject/object distinction from which the concept of the other—and hence of "being with others"—was supposed to have freed us. For Sartre the other becomes either another perceiving subject or else another perceived object, whereas there is a prior question as to the mode of spatialization through which gazes are distributed and discover their possible relations with one another—me in our eyes, you in mine; and that spatialization is itself not personal, not owned by either you or me. Thus Deleuze says that even when perceived as another person, *autrui* is in fact an impersonal possibility of perception—neither another subject nor another object but *personne* (no one), a "possible world" to be filled by you and me and the ways we appear to one another. And that is precisely what Tournier's experiment in fiction shows. What happens when the other is not there or is "foreclosed" from possible experience is a "destructuring" or "ungrounding" that affects at once the perceiving subject and the perceptual field; other kinds of movement and form emerge no longer fixed as definite objects given to unchanging subjects. In particular we see a loss of Gestaltist or phenomenological perceptual organization such as the relations between figure and ground, profile and unity, center and margin, length and depth, horizon and focus, up and down; and Tournier's solitary hero journeys to a strange new sense of the Earth, prior to the heaven/hell relation even in its Sartrian version. The induction is then that this Earth subsists in all the geometries of our lives, all our relations with one another. Tournier's tale shows that *autrui* is not a subject or an object but a principle of the spatial dispositions of our being together, which can itself become undone, exposing a potential for "other geometries." The problem changes. Being seen even voyeuristically is not after all a matter of a primal shame or identity anxiety. Instead of the great duel of gazes in the café, one confronts what happens when the perceptual system itself loosens up, allowing other things to happen. There arises the new problem of spaces of possible "encounter" not rooted in the futilities of the search for recognition, but concerned instead with the play of other possible worlds.

Let's take some other examples. Deleuze thinks that a problem of "faciality" arises once the face is extracted from the role assigned to it by classical perspective, in particular in paintings of Christ.[3] In Francis Bacon's painting the body loses its face in a great effort to attain another mode of "spatialization" in which figures appear in relation to one another in such a way as to "illustrate" nothing—no story that may be told in advance, no image already recorded or known, existing in some "imaginary museum."[4] But this faceless condition is an extreme case of something we already see in another way in the fiction of Marcel Proust, in relation to Albertine, where jealousy becomes a way of generating other possible worlds that threaten to spin out from between the cracks or interstices of the stratified world of nineteenth-century Paris.[5] The problem is put in yet another form in the New World setting of Herman Melville's fiction. There the modern dilemma of "being without qualities" becomes a problem of finding a space in which to be together yet each an "original"—a search for the sort of dynamic space that Ralph Waldo Emerson had already called "the highway," without which New World differences would fall back into what we today would call an "identity war."[6] In both cases one may observe that the "architecture" of the novel is transformed to accommodate the freer, less structured geometries of its characters, just as through Bacon's flattened pictorial "constructions" his figures appear in a free disposition no longer "illustrative" of anything.

We may then infer that through a loosening in "plan" or in "construction," the other geometries subsisting in our lives are released. But it is true as well in the idea of possible worlds that Leibniz introduced into philosophy. For, as Michel Serres has argued, this idea was inseparable from a new conception of *mundus* or the world, no longer subordinated to the *cosmos*, decentered and perspectival, as in baroque art or Elizabethan drama contemporary with it.[7] Deleuze believes that this problem of a world expressed at once in many perspectives assumes a new shape in modern works, where one finds a space that is not simply uncentered or without any overarching point of view, but without the need for a preestablished harmony among the various perspectives. The problem of *autrui*, of being with others, then becomes one of constructing spaces owned by no one, allowing disparate points of view to coexist in the absence of any "architectonic" system or harmony.

What, it may be asked, do these literary, pictorial, or philosophical ideas of "geometries of living" not drawn from prior points of a system such as Albertian perspective or traditional narrative have to do with the sort of thing that Euclid thought he was studying when he invented his axiomatic system of pure or ideal mathematical figures—an invention that so impressed the young Plato as to count as a source of his very image of philosophical thought? We thus come to a second philosophical problem, also very traditional: How are geometries and therefore "other geometries" *known*? How do they figure in our experience?

Intuition
In Euclid's geometry, philosophers found a whole model of knowledge, sometimes developing it along lines of their own, as with Spinoza's notion of ethics as a geometry of affects. Geometry was thought a model of necessary, eternal truth; the very "architecture" of

Wittgenstein's *Tractatus* still bears witness to it. The problem of geometry thus has a long and complicated history, which, as Serres points out, is in some sense coextensive with the history of philosophy itself and its entanglements with roles both practical and metaphysical that "geometry" assumed in the arts—or again in politics. One problem concerns what Euclid's figures have to do with our "ordinary" or everyday experience of geometry—with the geometries of the "life-world." Many people are inclined to think that Euclid sets the true sense of geometry, and that the literary or pictorial investigations of geometries of living are at best derived analogies. Plato himself thought sensory objects to be the imperfect copies of such ideal figures. But in modern philosophy we find some influential dissent from such Platonism.

Let's take two cases. The first is Wittgenstein; he says that Plato's problem of the relation between an ideal Euclidean figure like a circle and a real one it is used to describe, say a wheel, is a false problem—one we need to dissolve rather than solve. For in fact we are dealing with two different "language games," each useful in its own way, neither the basis of the other. One might even say that the two games belong to different "forms of life"; and Wittgenstein insists that we look more closely at exactly how geometries come to be learned and used. For example, we might ask just how and what one was supposed to learn to build from geometries contained in Paul Klee's "pedagogical sketchbooks" at the Bauhaus. The example is not arbitrary, for Wittgenstein had a complicated relation with drawing and architecture, and in fact came to give the lectures advancing his practice-minded, anti-Platonist remarks on mathematics following his work on the design of his sister's villa.[8]

Another departure from Platonism in modern philosophy comes from Edmund Husserl, who develops his idea of "phenomenology" out of an early study of the intuitive origins of numbers. Phenomenology is supposed to get us away from the "natural attitude." It says that what is real is in fact the lived everyday experience of space and that Euclid's abstract figures, far from giving the "real" basis of that experience, are only something derived from it for certain purposes. It is the task of phenomenology to describe such "lived experience" of space; from it, one learns of a grounded, situated body or "flesh" moving within the sort of figure/ground, horizon/center relations that may be supposed by "the other" in our experience—a bodily spatialization of the world also explored in painting, for example, in the "thingness" of Cézanne's apples. Thus we may say that the phenomenological or lived space of a house or a city is quite different from the abstract geometrical one obtained from mathematics alone. We find many versions of this idea. Henri Lefebvre is not alone in trying to derive from it a critical view of modern architecture and urbanism, resulting in his well-known disapproval of "abstract space." In a late book on the origins of geometry, Husserl himself talks about "vague essences" prior to what can be constructed through Euclidean geometric figures, indeterminate, given through informal intuition—for example, a "roundness" prior to any ideal circularity. This idea of indeterminate essences given informally yet with an "anexact" rigor is one that appeals to Deleuze, who sees in them something akin to the free, errant lines in Klee's sketchbooks. Deleuze finds it too bad that Husserl introduces the idea only as a means of showing the "origins" of ideal figures; for instead of a "protogeometry," such essences might be developed on their own—we might say as an "other" or "alternative" geometry.[9]

Wittgenstein and Husserl both participate in a larger philosophical controversy initiated toward the end of the last century, about the same time as the emergence of modern architecture, concerned with the "foundations of mathematics"—with what numbers and figures are and how they are "built up," from logic or from intuition. The controversy—one of the most important since the Greeks—would have a number of bifurcations. Alan Turing helped start the fork that leads to our contemporary paradigm of cognition and artificial intelligence, when, beginning with a model of a computing machine, he arrived at a result equivalent to Gödel's incompleteness theorem. Today his problems of "simulation" and of form and memory as an intelligence working in machines as in living beings has become the stuff of wired pop culture. Another fork, now mostly forgotten by philosophers, was taken by Alfred North Whitehead. After working out *Principia Mathematica* with Bertrand Russell, Whitehead went on to raise the question of geometry in a world of "process" or "becoming," as it had been raised in a tradition of "alternative cosmologies" starting with Plato himself when he talked of a *chora*—a sort of receptacle or sieve prior to the eternal Forms and their grip on matter. Among those concerned with the "foundations of mathematics" at the turn of the century, Whitehead ventures out again on the "minor" epistemological tradition including Stoic physics and Leibnizian metaphysics, to which Deleuze and Serres would later return and which some today see revived in the speculations surrounding systems of complexity or self-organization.

In this minor tradition of "geometries of becoming," the problem of geometry and its relation to literary or pictorial spatial investigation tends to be posed in a certain way. It is as if Husserl's "vague essences" had become the object of a geometry focused on concrete problems rather than concerned to derive everything from axioms, closer to engineers than to academics, dealing with sensations and bodies—a geometry of "affective space." For speculations in this tradition share a concern for indeterminate essences prior to contoured rectilinear ones, for dynamic or "emergent" properties rather than fixed or static ones, and an appeal to intuition with its anexact rigor rather than to the calculations of set theory as the way to capture the nondenumerable multiplicity or complexity that such essences or properties suppose. This intuitive or informal grasp of "geometries of becoming" in turn tends to attract literary or artistic interest or "translation," as if fiction or image might get at them through other means. Thus with Bergson's philosophy arises an art or literature of fluidity and movement, exemplified, say, by Virginia Woolf, just as later, along with Henry James, there would be a "stream of consciousness" fiction, or following Whitehead, the "entropic" spaces of Robert Smithson. Serres selects the word *translation* to refer to such relations between sciences and arts; he tries to work out, for example, the "translations" between notions of indetermination in thermodynamics and in the new "sublimity" in pictorial space found in J. M. W. Turner. Deleuze was also drawn to such relations, developing them along original lines, constructing relations for example between Leibnizian monads and baroque drama, or Bergsonian duration and new wave film. He came to think that there is no philosophy worth the name without this kind of translation in arts or sciences; such indeed was his experience with his own philosophy, when he opened his seminar to an "open" public following '68 in the "alternative" campus of Vincennes.

"Other geometries" thus require other ways of knowing that don't fit the Euclidean model. They are given by intuition rather than deduction, by informal diagrams or maps that incorporate an element of free indetermination rather than ones that work with fixed overall structures into which one inserts everything. Indeed without such intuitive knowledge or informal diagrams, they might well go unseen or unactualized. Thus it is not so much that there exists a nice grounded, phenomenological everyday experience or lived spatiality as the source of ideal geometric figures, or that the languages of scientific and ordinary geometries are learned and applied according to different rules or within different forms of life. It is rather that there exist other unnoticed, less determinate, structured or systematic spatializations, which may be explored at once through specific scientific and artistic investigation. The rule of the relation between the two is that neither is privileged and that translations are only worth the effects they have within the specific domain into which translation is made. But what might this mean for the specific domain of built or tectonic space? Which is more important for the geometries of building, Euclid or Virginia Woolf?

Form

In particular, what might architecture make of the minor tradition sketched above concerning the geometries of becoming? One suggestion comes from Greg Lynn, based in a contrast with Colin Rowe's "mathematics of the ideal villa" and its destiny in the "formalist" approaches to built space.[10] Rowe's study draws on an attempt by Rudolf Wittkower to isolate a nine-square grid as the hidden ideal type capable of generating all of Palladio's villas without being found as such in any single one. Rowe extends this analysis to Le Corbusier's villas Savoye and Stein, despite all differences in historical period and context. Rowe later repents, turning instead to a model of collage or bricolage among existing elements celebrated as a sort of complexity or heterogeneity.[11] Lynn suggests that we revisit this itinerary today from the standpoint of what he calls "alternative mathematics."

Alternative mathematics is different from the mathematics that inspired Wittkower and then Rowe. It is an informal mathematics of the singular with its open-ended variability or iterability rather than a deductive mathematics of the general with its particular variants. Thus instead of trying to find an "ideal villa" of which real ones would be the variants, one tries to map indeterminate or informal variations from singular points, leading to other possible paths, shapes, movements. One thinks in terms not of a hidden ideal villa but of an unseen "virtual" villa, the diagram of which, when superimposed on a space, would singularize it, open it, making it at once more multiple, flexible and unpredictable.

Lynn's point may then be put in this way: Rowe's turn to collage and complexity makes sense only in contrast with the reductive formalism of the ideal villa that he abandoned. But the mathematics of virtual movement and shape suggests another sort of "formalism" that may be seen in other places in the work of Le Corbusier—for example in his collaboration with Xenakis, his composer-engineer, on the Philips Pavilion. This formalism is closer to Klee's free lines than to Kandinsky's spiritual figures—to a dynamic sense of the relations between movement and plan. For in a certain sense the classical Palladian villa and the modern ones patterned on it, precisely to the degree that they tend to subordinate all specificity to invariant perfect types, keep everything in place, anticipate and so preclude surprise, chance, encounter—just the sorts of thing that an alternative mathematics might help bring out. Paul Virilio, for example, has argued that the geometry of this classical space supposes a static body, unfit for the dynamic trajectories that modern transport would help introduce into living, producing an intensity in movement better served by topological models or choreographic notations— by different, more affective geometries, closer to the grounded phenomenological flesh. The more intuitive or informal schemes of an alternative mathematics then allow us to raise another, less "reductive" question about form. They ask what can be *done* with form once it is released from "classical" determination within a field or ground, when it is no longer given to an external or overseeing eye accustomed to nice up-down, vertical-horizontal structures or some "collage" among them. That is what I will call the problem of "operative form."

Let's take a related debate in painting or drawing. There now exists an abundant literature contesting Albertian perspective as something basic to pictorial space or pictorial composition. Thus in *Discours, figure*, Jean-François Lyotard tries to work out another principle of spatial composition, no longer offered to the self-certainty of an external perspectival eye, working instead through a kind of informal "matrix" generative of other, less fixed types of figures or forms.[12] His theme is that the resulting "figural" space has a different relation than does the Albertian "figurative" one to affect, intuition, discourse—to what can and cannot be seen or said. There is a "figurality" or "plasticity" of space that *works* on us in a different way than by offering figurative contents, which Lyotard likens to the workings of the whole scenography of the Freudian dreams. But the notion that pictorial space works or operates in another way than representing objects or illustrating stories has an interest that goes beyond the specific parallels with the Freudian dream work. For it involves a "formlessness" that is not itself another content to be shown by slightly distorted of distended forms but rather an operative condition that allows forms or figures to *do* other things, to affect us in other ways. The passage to this free or formless space prior to classical figures and stories does not lie in a reduction to a purity of means of representation; there exist many other paths to it, many other results of it. We might thus talk of an "operative" rather than a "reductive" or "purifying" formalism, where the issue is not what forms mean or represent but what they do, what they *can* do.

Everyone is familiar in architecture with the kind of abstraction that tries to isolate form or figure from context or milieu or else index it on a single variable taken in isolation like function or structure. Form is then valued for its autonomy, its independence from matter or "content"—the more autonomous, the more pure, the better. Alternative geometries suggest that there also exists another kind of abstraction based not on isolating form, celebrating its purity or autonomy, but, on the contrary, on releasing it from the sort of spatial system that defines and fixes shapes, organizes visibility, ensuring there will be no surprises, of which Albertian perspective and Wittkowerian "ideal villas" would count as examples. Such abstraction works according to another principle. Reductive or purifying abstraction tends to the religion of the blank canvas, the empty page or tabula rasa. The principle of operative abstraction is instead that it is just when a spatial construction is loosened up, when it becomes less "systematic" (more incomplete or "formless"), that its forms or figures become more singular, more original, free to behave in other, less predictable ways or affect us along other, less direct lines. The problem of other geometries is then how to introduce this anorganized or complex space into building—in other words how to create a free, operative space in construction not preset by any overarching organization or given through combination among existing elements.

We have already seen how certain novels or paintings work in this way, loosening their constructions to allow for other "geometries of living." There is a change in their "architecture"; it becomes at once less systematic and more plastic, allowing other sorts of things to happen. Thus the "violence" through which Bacon frees his figures from the ambient world of photographic cliché to move in other less "probable" ways that illustrate nothing requires the invention of another space of movement, connected to a strange plasticity of the body, expressed through an original sort of pictorial construction. It is the same in the novel. In Proust, as "the other" becomes "expression of possible world," the space of the novel opens up to include "complicated time" through which those worlds unfold, emerging out of the *mondanités* of Parisian life. Similarly Melville's invention of the "original" character introduces an intense dynamic space that frees narrative structure from the "neurotic" rationalities of plot traditional in the British or French novel, pointing to the more "schizophrenic," Borgesian situation where characters become so flexible or indeterminate that at any point they might bifurcate and go off into other possible narratives.

Of course, the search for "mobility" in Melville's law office is different from the search for "lost time" in Proust's Paris; and both differ from the new forces diagnosed through the black humor of the institutional spaces of Franz Kafka's *Mitteleuropa*. Yet in their different settings they raise a problem of what it means to exist "without qualities" or to attain a free space released from any "qualified existence." In a "meditation" on the typical plan, Rem Koolhaas has recently tried to formulate this problem of "being without qualities" as an architectural proposition.[13] With a characteristic touch of perversity, he says something like this: if you want to get an idea of a New World space so "smooth" that all particular qualities slip off it, go take another look at the World Trade Center or the RCA Building in New York City. For there in a business setting is to be found something more akin to Melville's loose, uncemented incomplete wall than the endless corridors of Kafka's *Castle* or the off-on switches of Godard's *Alphaville*—a space of "no one" yet not a space of anomie. For many eyes such typical-plan buildings are the very epitome of reductive minimalism in architecture, of abstract Euclidean space. In asking us to see them instead as "formless," Koolhaas touches on the problem of an operative abstraction that departs from decoration and sculpture in another way than through reduction or purification—one that asks what can be *done* through form when it is free to move within a looser, more flexible, less predicable sort of arrangement, once it starts to move in an affective space.

The Virtual
So where are we? We started our excursion with the problem of other geometries of living and the role of construction in certain novels or paintings in bringing them out; we then looked at a minor tradiion of a mathematics of indefinite shape and virtual movement given

through intuitive diagram. The two were brought together in the problem of operative form. For when form is no longer determined by a prior field or ground given to an independent or overseeing eye, it starts to operate in other, less systematic or predictable ways. The problem then becomes one of loosening up construction so as to "singularize" a space, disposing it in a free manner not completely organized or determined. This problem in turn leads to questions about the very nature of the powers and potentials of built space—to the whole question of "the virtual" in construction and the idea of a "pure" or indeterminate "immanence" in it of what is yet possible to be and do.

Let me suggest what I have in mind by coming back to the architecture of Peter Eisenman and his ambition to build in such a way as to challenge prevailing conventions or rules of building. I'll end with a small observation about the different descriptions under which that ambition is carried out. It seems to me that the early houses work with a model of autonomy, abstraction, and critical self-reference, but already with his "artificial cities," with their Piranesian affinities, new sorts of questions emerge concerning a more "grounded" condition. Perhaps the current interest in "other geometries" belongs to a third phase, with a "smoother," less disjointed look, in which the very idea of self-critical formalism erodes even further. For in the end, that idea of autonomy and the formalism that goes with it only make sense within a certain conception of the geometries of built space. In challenging that conception in turn, the question becomes not simply one of operative rather than autonomous form, but also and at the same time of another image of critical intervention in architecture beyond abstract purity or transgressive gesture. In Eisenman's continuing architectural voyage we would thus see enacted a complex passage from a "critical" or self-referential to a "virtual" or operative conception of the space of thought and intervention. In this passage perhaps lie the most powerful connections to be forged between this work and the philosophical problems that this essay has sought to bring out.

What is the problem of "future cities" or "cities of the future?" What does critical thought and so critical architectural intervention have do with it?

The relation of cities to the future belongs to the conditions, the very idea of critical thought. Maybe there can be no thought without some critical relation to the future, some resistance to the present. Even the sad little ironies of our now fading postmodernism offer unwitting proof of this. Many sorts of images of this "other future" have been invented, utopian and dystopian, transgressive and cynical. They vary with different images of time (progressive, nostalgic, linear, circular, etc.) as well as with notions of how and to whom the "other future" is given. As such they go back to the very idea of the *polis*— of the city, of "the political." But what is *their* future today?

One idea, "virtual futures," supposes a view of a time that can go "out of joint" as the time peculiar to the city, and says that unjointed times precede our given iden-tities, our possible relations with one another. It is thus concerned with invisibility—with an "imperceptibility" of our becomings. In effect, it says that invisible cities are critical, that is, diagnostic of what is to come, just when they are "virtual," and converse-ly that the virtual futures of cities are always invisible, since their actualizations always involve a departure from known or foreseeable identities. A *seven* condition of critical thought then is that our future be as yet unforesee-able and our past yet to be determined, and hence that at no one time can we completely know or master or plan who we are or may be-come. Future cities may then be said to be those invented, imagined, "construct-ed" relations or pas-sageways between this unforeseen future and this indetermi-nate past in our being, through which

we respond to the necessity, in what is happening to us, of some event— of some "actualiza-tion" in the present of a virtual future. What role might architecture or architectural in-tervention play in such future cities —such out-of-joint inventions and self-inventions of our virtual futures?

Today we face two problems, re-lated to one an-other in complex ways, often difficult to separate from one another: how to get away from certain utopian or transgressive images of thought—or the "future" of thought—and envisage other modes of critical intervention and critical analysis; and how to develop a new conception or image of cities, their shapes, their distinctive problems, the ways in which they figure in our being and being-together, the manner in which they acquire their identities, the kinds of movement they introduce within and among us—an image that would still allow for the play of critical invention and intervention. In asking what architecture might still do to surprise us in the cities of the future, we may then distinguish two lines of debate.

Line 1: Today we see urbanization on a massive scale and in a global setting; by 2025 more than two-thirds of the world's population will be concentrated in urban areas.[1] This poses all kinds of new problems, demographic, ecological, political. It is not simply a question of megacities like São Paulo and Tokyo. In some ways the whole idea of "city" is changing. The greatest and most rapid change is in developing countries, where every day the overall urban population increases by 150,000, often outstripping local resources. Such massive processes include the new patterns of immigration that have already transformed older metropolises, once the centers of colonial empire, and are inseparable from the creation of a "new poverty" that increasingly paralyzes these countries. Will cities assume a shape different from the urban sprawl of North America? Often cities of the new Asia are taken as offering another image, the shape of cities in the future. It is not always a comforting image; no one knows for sure how it is going to turn out.

This massive urbanization is global in some sense of that now ubiquitous buzzword. It supposes new relations with the local that transform our sense of region and therefore of critical regionalism. Some see a set of connections more "omnipolitan" than cosmopolitan, which

define a global business "city," together with a city of
real-time electronic-entertainment culture, coexisting in
many "places" at the same time, for which shopping supplies the main program. The new poverty, the new
immigration, then constitutes those denied citizenship in
this global city. The city seeks to protect itself from this
population, sometimes even to protect itself from *seeing*.
How should we analyze such processes? The sociology
or the discourses on modernity that we inherit from the
last century are still patterned on superimposing the
relations between Europe and antiquity on those
between the modern and traditional worlds. But perhaps
we now face new problems that may retrospectively
determine our sense of what the great European, and
then American and Russian, "modernizations" (and
therefore urbanizations) were in fact about. Thus the
Europe-America axis of the modernist avant-garde no
longer seems to play such a pivotal role in our cultural
geography—other kinds of climate, territory, history,
actors, perhaps even of "universality" are involved.

In this situation, what might a "critical architecture"
still do? What guises might it yet assume? Rem Koolhaas
gives a stark rhetorical answer: "none." The city of the
future will be "scraped of architecture" as we have
known it, and we need to invent something like a
"postarchitectural" style of intervention. The whole idea
of critical urban intervention must be rethought accord-
ingly. We must question assumptions about the identity
and context of cities and the ideological assumptions of
analyzing and intervening in them. In particular,
Koolhaas argues that the real determinants of the spatial
"arrangement" or "assemblage" of cities (and so of
movement in cities) no longer conform to the archaeo-
logical model of accumulating layers on a more or less
centered "historical" site, of which the great European

metropolises are examples, thus turning their preserva-
tion into a dilemma. Instead of lamenting or trying to
repair this fact, we should direct our urbanistic imagination to the other real determinants of cities: we should
pay more attention to infrastructure than to context in
the analysis of cities and so of the other possibilities of
cities—that is, of the future cities or invisible cities that
we might yet dream up.

This dramatic image of the postarchitectural city
may help focus debate. What are the real determinants
of the cities of the future or the cities of the new Asia?
What should be done about residual context? What
possibilities do they open up? What kinds of odd movement do they restrict or permit? What do they suppose
about so-called globalization? And what sort of architectural intervention can we thus envisage in them? In
what ways do they offer new settings for invention,
release, experiment with our virtual futures and therefore with ourselves in them?

Line 2: The notions of "invisibility" and "future"
have long been linked in the traditions of philosophy,
hence of critical thought; one may thus say that an "art
of seeing" belongs to what it is to think.[2] A turning point
arises when the future and the city's given "identity" are
no longer thought to be compatible or congruent. The
future then becomes "invisible" in a particular sense: its
"image" no longer stands in any representational relation
with the real cities from which it derives; it has a prob-
lematizing rather than an idealizing relation with them.
The appeal to a "future people" or a "people to come"
made by certain writers supplies one example: this other
people who must learn to speak a foreign language,
which Proust thought might emerge from the stratifica-
tions of nineteenth-century Paris; or again the "other
people" prior to the public/private distinction, linked to

diabolical forces knocking at the door, whose power for Kafka is that of a "minor language" in German. The principle of such other, invisible, future peoples is not some recognition withheld by a state or its majority. Rather, we can invent the other peoples that we already are or may become as singular beings only if our being and being-together are indeterminate—not identifiable, given, recognizable in space and time—in other words, if our future remains unknown and our past indeterminate such that our very narratives can go out of joint, exposing other histories in our histories, releasing the strange powers of an artifice in our very "nature." Fiction and cinema have both explored the powers, the times, the spaces of this principle of the future city. What would it mean to introduce it into the specific kind of spaces in which architects have traditionally worked? What would it mean to make it an irreducible part of "construction?"

The
problem
can be put in
this way: the virtual
house is the one which,
through its plan, space, construction, and intelligence, gener-
ates the most new connections, the one
so arranged or disposed as to permit the
greatest power for unforeseen relations. But what
is this idea of the virtual as multiple potentials for new
connections or unseen relations?

A starting point lies in the distinction drawn by the philosopher Gilles Deleuze between the virtual
and the possible, or the actualization of
the virtual and the realization of the possible. It is part of a larger attempt to
understand the notion of potential outside the given identities of
form, function, and place, and it leads to the following principle:
the world that is best is the most "multiple," the most virtual.

The problem of the virtual house may then also be put this
way: it is the one that most catches us by surprise in our very
manners of thinking and being. Perhaps the strongest modernist
works have done this in their own way, but that doesn't mean that
the virtual house should look like any of them or repeat their
manifestos. In fact, the virtual looks like *nothing* we already know
or can see. The aim of this description is thus not to say what the
virtual house should resemble, represent, or symbolize; that, by
definition, is not possible. It is rather to try to formulate some
questions implicated in the idea of the virtual house.

Concept

The idea of the virtual is quite old. The word comes from *virtus*,
meaning potential or force, and often comes coupled with the
actual, meaning that through which the potential or force
becomes at once visible and effective. As such it names one of the
oldest problems in philosophy: it was involved in the very ideas of

oikos, polis, ethos (home, city, manner of being). Long after Aristotle, Leibniz and Bergson would take it up again. Deleuze takes up the arrow in turn, launching it in a new direction. To actualize the virtual, he says, is not the same as to realize the possible, and it is crucial not to confuse the two.[1] In a phrase taken from Proust, the virtual is "real without being actual, ideal without being abstract." It thus acquires a power of a peculiar kind calling for a special kind of intelligence.

The actual is then what manifests and effectuates the virtual, but the actual never *completely* shows or activates all that the virtual implies. Something always remains. For Bergson, for example, the virtual is the force of the past always still with us in the present, yet to be actualized, unfolding in our lives beyond what we are able to recollect or recognize. The virtual lies in those forces or potentials whose origins and outcomes cannot be specified independently of the open and necessarily incomplete series of their actualizations. Such is their multiplicity (or complexity) that it can never be reduced to a set of discrete elements or to the different parts of a closed or organic whole. (This is what Bergson called "qualitative" rather than "quantitative" multiplicity.)

The virtual is thus not an abstraction, a generality, or an a priori condition. It doesn't take us from the specific to the generic. It increases possibility in another way: it mobilizes as yet unspecifiable singularities, bringing them together in an indeterminate plan. How we are to conceive of, and therefore deal with, potentials or forces that depart from the possibilities of given forms, structures, or ideas, affecting us in ways that go beyond what we can wholly grasp and working in other ways than through overall organizations or blueprints?

The actual and the virtual are thus not logically congruent or commensurable. Actualization is never in the image of the virtual force it effectuates. Unlike the possible, whose realization always leaves us the same, the virtual is something we must always experiment and work with in order to see. It confronts us as a question or problem to which we don't know how to respond in advance. We don't know yet how to react to it since it falls under no available description. Deleuze thinks that the "time images" of postwar film are virtual in this sense: they make visible something intolerable for which there existed no preset manner of thinking.

What would it mean for the virtual to be part of the very idea of construction? Let's take Deleuze's Leibnizian account of the baroque house, where the real and the ideal no longer belong to different realms but inhabit the same uncentered perspectival "possible world"—the very world that God has selected as best. Perhaps we today no longer need Leibniz's postulate of compossibility among different perspectives nor, therefore, the baroque idea of a God who has already selected. A neo-Leibnizian definition of the virtual house might then be this: it is the house that holds together the most, and most complicated, "different possible worlds" in the same container, allowing them to exist together along a constructed plane with no need of a preestablished harmony.

Smart Houses

Smart machines are different from dynamic or mechanical ones. Unlike the locomotive devices like the airplane or the car that interested Marinetti and Le Corbusier, here information moves instead of the body. Thus these smart machines help create new spaces of body and mind. Their impact on architecture has not yet been resolved. So far we have been presented solely with a kind of programmatic progressivism or futurism difficult to separate from marketing hype and promotion. The problem is usually posed in terms of a virtual space where bits are called upon to do what was formerly done by atoms, creating invisible cities patterned on the real ones that they at once simulate and displace. The virtual house might then mean one of two things: it might mean a house wired for home automation, equipped to sense, serve, and protect the body—what Paul Virilio calls the "handicapped body." Bill Gates's house is an extravagant advertisement for this. The problem it raises is that of architecture in smart environments according to a model where the environment is a batch of bits and the architectural unit is the computer or mind that processes them. Or again, the virtual house might mean the house on the screen according to the paradigm in which one talks of virtual libraries, museums, or shopping centers. Apart from the obsolescence of the simulated functions, this raises certain architectural problems: that of images no longer framed by walls or anchored in tectonic space but floating, moving as though pieces of information on a screen; and more generally the problem of a less grounded sense of the body and movement. Instead of a house for an insulated, handicapped body aided by machines that do everything it wants, the virtual house becomes here the house of this less grounded condition of image and body, as though it were a house for an unreal, disembodied mind linked to all others in a virtual realm.

But are these the only possibilities for architectural thought or intervention in the "age of smart machines?" Do there not exist other, less comforting, less automatic potentials not patterned on simulation and interactivity that the sense of the virtual developed here might bring out?

The virtual house is a special sort of machine with an "artifice" or "intelligence" that is not wholly informational. For the virtual is not another unreal realm that only doubles or "simulates" the nature we already know or see. Rather it supposes something singular yet to be constructed in the arrangements that determine our nature. To virtualize nature is thus not to double it but, on the contrary, to multiply it, complicate it, release other forms and paths in it. The virtual house might therefore be very smart after all, even delirious, while remaining perfectly real.

Virtual Construction

A virtual construction is one that frees forms, figures, and activities from a prior determination or grounding, of the sort they have, for example, in classical Albertian perspective, allowing them to function or operate in other unanticipated ways; the virtuality of a space is what gives such freedom in form or movement. Thus virtual construction departs from organizations that try to set out all possibilities in advance. It constructs a space whose rules can themselves be altered through what happens in it. But how then can there be such a thing as a "virtual plan?"

The usual way to increase possibility is to abstract from specificity, thus finding something more generalized. Increased possibility comes at the price of reducing specificity. The house with the most possibilities might thus seem the one with the least specificities—the empty house, the house of silence or absence, awaiting a revelation that never comes. The virtual house is not like that. Its arrangement or disposition allows for the greatest number of singular points, the most complex connections made from them. If the virtual house is not completely specified by fixed qualities, it is because it is a dynamic space prior to any qualifications—so "smooth" that fixed qualities do not stick to it, are always slipping off it. Its geometry is not drawn from fixed points. The virtual functions by multiplying, by throwing together singular points and seeing what they can do. Thus it inserts chance where there was only probability.

The ruse of the possible is to make it seem that outside the aegis of the specifiable all is illogical, unplannable, ineffable—pure anarchy, disorder, chaos, irrationality. As if the only powers were those of organization, determination; as if there didn't exist potentials of another sort, working according to another kind of plan. One way out of the suffocating sense of too much programmed, instrumentalized possibility has been a theology of the impossible, a mysticism of the unsayable and the invisible. But while voids, erasures, and absences can of course all be used to help virtualize or singularize a specific space, the virtual plan is never obtained simply by emptying a space or via the *via negativa*. For it is after all a plan, not a primal void. The virtual plan is thus not a general, abstract, or master plan; yet neither is it an empty or deconstructed one, functioning by unbuilding, undoing, or collapse alone. It is free just because it is neither ideal nor impossible. That is why the virtual house is the most intense house, the one to most "affect" in ways that surprise us, obliging us to go beyond what normally seems possible.

Thinking Virtual
Architects have thought in terms of utopia and ideological program. They have thought in terms of transgression and formal play. The virtual introduces another style of thought. It has nothing to do with an ideology, a belief in an encompassing order, real or utopian. It thinks in terms of arrangements of body and soul, irreducible to any such symbolic order, any such law of possibilities. If it is critical, its critique does not consist in

saying "no" or transgressing a supposed order or pater-
nity. It says "no" only to affirm new possibilities through
a virtual construction that says "yes" as well as "and."

We already know the principle of this style of
thought: the more connections, more singular points
connected, the greater the "virtuality" of the resulting
arrangement. Already with Leibniz the "best world" is
not the perfect world but the one with the greatest virtuality; such is his baroque way of approaching a principle of selection and belief no longer based in divine
judgment or in a Judgment Day. For while he still supposes a division of the world into saved and damned, he
holds that the damned damn themselves by failing to
develop the virtuality of which they are capable. For a
principle of judgment he thus substitutes a principle of
"virtuality" in our manners of being, a jurisprudence of
the singular. Freed from Leibniz's lingering baroque salvationism, such is the principle of selection of the virtual
house: the one that keeps our possibilities, our hopes
from salvationism, and our impossibilities, our despair
from resignation.

These are some senses in which the virtual house
may be said to be the house that in its plan, space, construction, and intelligence gives the greatest number of
"new connections." But of course there is a problem. It
has yet to be designed.

One **Constructions**

1. See "Hume" in Gilles Deleuze, *Immanence—A Life: Essays in Empiricism* (New York: Zone Books, forthcoming).

2. Gilles Deleuze, *Critique et clinique* (Paris: Minuit, 1993), 40–42. Deleuze is the first to introduce this phrase into philosophy, saying that Hamlet rather than Oedipus, Shakespeare rather than Aeschylus, manages finally to "emancipate time" from given spaces of movement. The idea forms part of an original view of Kant's own oeuvre, according to which, in a last phase, the philosopher would have decided to let the rules of the faculties that he had previously been at **Notes** such pains to establish move in a free, unregulated space—a sort of *dérèglement de tous les sens*, pointing to what was to come. Kant is thus less "architectonic" than he thinks; Deleuze stresses that Kant already talks of the "orientation of thought," or in terms of territory and Earth.

3. Gilles Deleuze and Félix Guattari, *What Is Philosophy?* (New York: Columbia University Press, 1994), 186.

4. Ian Hacking stresses the role of chance and experiment in Peirce's philosophy in *The Taming of Chance* (Cambridge: Cambridge University Press, 1990); Hacking compares Peirce to Nietzsche, following Deleuze. I refer to the problem of chance in Peirce's "The Architecture of Theories" in my short contribution, "On Not Being Any One," in *Anyone*, ed. Cynthia Davidson (New York: Rizzoli, 1991).

5. Friedrich Nietzsche, *Thus Spoke Zarathustra* (Harmondsworth: Penguin, 1961), Book III, "Of the Spirit of Gravity," 213. See also "Of Old and

New Law-Tables" (226): "Human society, that is an experiment, so I teach . . . an experiment, O my brothers! And *not* a 'contract.'"

6. See Peter Galison, "Aufbau/Bauhaus: Logical Positivism and Architectural Modernism," *Critical Inquiry* 16 (Summer 1990). Galison's story might be continued. Positivist philosophy and functionalism in architecture both came to the United States, where they gained the acceptance they lacked in Europe. But it was not to last; during the Vietnam decade a reaction would set in against both. Thus already in the early 1960s we find Thomas Kuhn proposing a new "image of science" against the positivists and Robert Venturi advancing a new more "complex" rhetoric of architecture against the modernists; both in turn would be absorbed into postmodernism. Ray Monk relates the story of Loos and Wittgenstein in *Wittgenstein: The Duty of Genius* (London: Jonathan Cape, 1990). On Wittgenstein's house, see Paul Wijdeveld, *Ludwig Wittgenstein, Architect* (Cambridge: MIT Press, 1994).

7. In *Wittgenstein on Rules and Private Language* (Cambridge: Harvard University Press, 1982), Saul Kripke proposes to make the problem of "following a rule" central to Wittgenstein's private language argument. Thus the argument would be "skeptical," implying that rules are not only public but indeterminate—we cannot be sure just what the rules are of the predicates that define us. The nature of this indetermination is found as well in Nelson Goodman's "new paradox of induction," showing that prediction depends on "entrenched predicates." In this manner, Kripke rediscovers Hume and the problem of chance in our "constructions" of ourselves. Perhaps Goodman's conception of "world-making" is not so far from Deleuze's notion that the modern *work* is one with rules such that many "possible worlds" may exist together in the same "plan."

Two **Folding**
This essay first appeared as "Perplications: On the Space and Time of Rebstockpark," in the catalogue *Unfolding Frankfurt* (Berlin: Ernst & Sohn, 1991).

1. Gilles Deleuze, *Le pli: Leibniz et le baroque* (Paris: Minuit, 1988), 188.

2. Gilles Deleuze, *Spinoza: Practical Philosophy* (San Francisco: City Lights, 1988).

3. Gilles Deleuze, *Pourparlers* (Paris: Minuit, 1990), 219.

4. On Lacan and Clérambault's veils, see Joan Copjec, "The Sartorial Superego," *October* 50 (Fall 1989); on Lacan and baroque vision, see Jacques Lacan, *Encore, 1972–1973* (Paris: Seuil, 1975), 95ff., and Christine Buci-Glucksmann, *La folie du voir* (Paris: Galilée, 1987).

5. Deleuze, *Le pli*, 5.

6. Deleuze, *Pourparlers*.

7. Gilles Deleuze, *Différence et répétition* (Paris: Presses Universitaires de France, 1968), 324–330, 359–360.

8. Deleuze proposes to use the terms *virtual* and *virtuality* in a special way. With these terms, he is not referring to what architectural criticism calls "virtual space" or what Rowe also terms "illusionism" in architecture. On the other hand, what Deleuze calls "virtual" is not to be confused with what Silicon Valley has decided to call "virtual reality," even though it is part of Deleuze's view that virtuality, unlike possibility, is always real. Perhaps the closest term in Peter Eisenman's own idiom would be "immanence." Deleuze introduces his sense of the virtual in his *Bergsonism* (New York: Zone Books, 1988), 96–103, distinguishing it from the possible. "Virtuality" is not the "possibility" of something that might be "realized"; it is already real, and it does not stand in a representational or mimetic relation to what "actualizes" it. Rather, what is virtual is always a "multiplicity"; and it is actualized through a free or creative "divergence." This theme is further elaborated in *Différence et répétition* (269–276) in relation to Leibniz, before being taken up again in *Le pli*. In that work it is also linked to "perplication"; the "perplication of the Idea" is defined as its "problematic character and the reality of the virtual that it represents" (324).

9. *Tadao Ando: The Yale Studio and Current Works* (New York: Rizzoli, 1989), 19.

10. On the grid in Eisenman's early work see Rosalind Krauss, "Death of a Hermeneutic Phantom: Materialization of the Sign in the Work of Peter Eisenman," in *Peter Eisenman: Houses of Cards* (New York: Oxford University Press, 1987); see also her "Grids," in *The Originality of the Avant-Garde and Other Modernist Myths* (Cambridge: MIT Press, 1985); this book also includes two original essays on the index.

11. On the connection between contemporary museums and finance capital see Rosalind Krauss, "The Cultural Logic of the Late Capitalist Museum," *October* 54 (Fall 1990); the problem of banking and finance plays an important role in the analysis of capitalism that Deleuze proposes in collaboration with Félix Guattari, as well as in a short text "Postscriptum sur Les Sociétés de Contrôle" in *Pourparlers*. It would seem timely to analyze along these lines the centrality of the museum as a type in contemporary architecture.

12. Jacques Derrida, "Force et signification" in *L'écriture et la différence* (Paris: Seuil, 1967), 28. By "pure absence" Derrida means "not the absence of this or that—but the absence of everything, in which every presence is announced" (17). This text first appeared in *Critique* in 1963, at a time when Derrida was still trying to work out a phenomenological contrast between geometric and literary "ideality." It is a review of a book by Jean Rousset, a central figure among those who, referring to Heinrich Wölfflin and Rudolf Wittkower, tried to establish the existence of a "baroque age" in literature. In *Le pli* Deleuze refers on several occasions to Rousset, remarking that those who have written best about the baroque are those most skeptical of the category. Rousset's account of the attempts to discover a baroque age includes reference to the rediscovery of the English metaphysical poets and, in this sense, lends support to Geoffrey Bennington's impression that "Mannerist and Baroque buildings are to Venturi [in *Complexity and Contradiction in Architecture*] what the English Metaphysical Poets were to Eliot." In 1963 Derrida took Rousset's "baroquism" as only one instance of something called "the structuralist passion," and he went on to advance the more general argument that the attempt to find

"spatial" or "architectural" metaphors for literature is ultimately vain, since there is something inherent in "literary ideality" that "excludes" this sort of description "in principle" ("Force et signification," 29). After 1963 one of course finds in Derrida's continuing reflections a more complex (not to say baroque) discussion of the theme of absence, and the theme has an important part in his writings on the architecture of both Eisenman and Bernard Tschumi. Yet it might be argued that Derrida preserves from his early work the general problematic of the literary and the spatial, or the textual and the architectural. Deleuze, by contrast, is never motivated by a search for a phenomenological contrast between literary and geometric ideality; instead, he invents a singular kind of spatial idiom in philosophy, using it in his readings of literature. Thus, he comes to the view that there is a sense in which architecture, regarded as a "framing of territory," is the *art premier*.

13. Gilles Deleuze and Félix Guattari, *A Thousand Plateaus* (Minneapolis: University of Minnesota Press, 1987), 293.

Three **Lightness**
This essay was an attempt to introduce a concept of lightness through a special issue of *ANY* (no. 5, March/April 1994) prepared together with Greg Lynn. As Cynthia Davidson points out in her marginal notes, new concepts today tend to get "weighed down" in scholarly or avant-garde journals, without yet finding themselves on the Internet; thus the old tabloid print form of *ANY,* "neither academic, nor avant-garde, nor electronic, might offer the concept, at least for a time, the fresh air it needs to pursue the multiple odd paths of its attempting" (5).

1. Bernard Cache, *Earth Moves* (Cambridge: MIT Press, 1995).

2. Gilles Deleuze and Félix Guattari, *A Thousand Plateaus* (Minneapolis: University of Minnesota Press, 1987), 371ff. This plateau (361–374), which contrasts *gravitas* and *celeritas*, finds another "light" conception of the Earth within a "minor" tradition in physics and geometry. On the problem of the "lightness" of the Earth in Nietzsche, see ibid., 508–509, as well as Deleuze's essay "Ariadne's Mystery," *ANY* 5 (March/April 1994).

3. Jacques Derrida, *The Ear of the Other* (Lincoln: University of Nebraska Press, 1988), 169. The reference is to the "joyous disturbance" introduced by "certain women's movements" within "our small European space." Nevertheless it is curious that Derrida ends his lecture on Nietzsche's ear by saying that "no woman or trace of woman, if I have read correctly" (38), since the whole question of ears and affirmation turns on the figure of Ariadne to whom Nietzsche has Dionysus singing: "You have my ears: Put a clever word into them! . . . I am your labyrinth." Deleuze draws attention to Ariadne as the persona of "redoubled affirmation" in Nietzsche's philosophy: see his "Ariadne's Mystery," as well as "Nietzsche" in *Immanence—A Life: Essays in Empiricism* (New York: Zone Books, forthcoming).

4. *El Croquis* (Madrid), no. 53 (1991).

5. Friedrich Nietzsche, *Thus Spoke Zarathustra*, Book III, "On the Spirit of Gravity" (Harmondsworth: Penguin, 1961), 211.

6. Martin Heidegger, "The Origin of the Work of Art," in *Poetry, Language, Thought* (New York: Harper, 1971), 42.

7. Husserl's essay on the Earth first appeared in Marvin Farber, *Philosophical Essays in Memory of Edmund Husserl* (Cambridge: Harvard University Press, 1940); it appears in French translation with a series of related fragments from the Husserl archives in Louvain under the title *La terre ne se meut pas* (Paris: Minuit, 1989). Didier Franck stresses that in these writings we see a conception of "flesh" prior to "all physics and all geometry," based rather in a kinesthetics of the body.

8. Nietzsche, *Thus Spoke Zarathustra*, Book III. These were thus the last words of the first version of the work, before the addition of Book IV.

9. Mary Wigman, "The Philosophy of Modern Dance," in *What Is Dance?*, ed. Roger Copeland and Marshall Cohen (New York: Oxford University Press, 1983), 306–307. On the question of dancing and building see the essays by Paul Virilio and Heidi Gilpin in *ANY* 5 (March/April 1994).

Four **Abstraction**
This essay first appeared as "Another View of Abstraction," in
Journal of Visual Arts, December 1994.

1. See Thierry de Duve, "The Monochrome and the Blank
Canvas," in his *Kant after Duchamp* (Cambridge: MIT Press,
1996). De Duve has analyzed different ways in which the problem of painting and the "pictorial" continues to haunt works that
are supposed to follow its death or end, even and especially those
said to be "antiaesthetic" or "anartistic," going back to
Duchamp. In this essay, de Duve focuses on the moment "after
abstract expressionism" when a sense of "art" and "artist"
emerges that no longer makes reference to any specific medium;
he connects the turn to some remarks of Barnett Newman, very
much in the negative-theological mode, and to Mallarmé,
declaring that he himself continues to be "seduced" by the
Mallarmean scheme. To understand the turn to art-in-general,
he thus proposes to extend the "privilege" or "lead" of painting
beyond the point to which Greenberg in effect took it: the blank
canvas. For painting on canvas is no more "essential" to the
medium than illusionist depth; indeed it is a relatively recent
convention, linked to a freeing of the pictorial object from its
ambient architecture. Why not, therefore, continue the monochromatic reduction of abstraction by other means, abandoning
the canvas itself and opening other ways of naming the pictorial?

2. See Lacan's seminar on ethics (Jacques Lacan, *The Ethics of
Psychoanalysis, 1959–1960* [New York: Norton, 1992]); I discuss
this view of sublimation in my *Truth and Eros: Foucault, Lacan,
and the Question of Ethics* (New York: Routledge, 1991), 71–76.
There is of course a Heideggerian element in this notion of primal emptiness or lack, and perhaps one might thus distinguish,
in Japanese traditions, the negative theology of Nishida and the
Kyoto School from the arts and practices of *ma* (the interval). In
any case, Roland Barthes likens the space and time of *ma* (and
not the great void) to Cy Twombly's wisdom in introducing into
pictorial space a sense of time or event quite different from
mythical narrative or theatricality, shown rather through a "scattered" sort of space (*espace épars*). For such space is not the result

of dispersing something enclosed, grounded, or totalized, leaving one with simple disorder; it is rather an existing, anorganized virtuality, subsisting in the intervals of enclosures, grounds, and totalities, through which to attain, says Barthes, what Nietzsche calls the "lightness" of things. Thus Twombly's scattered spaces have something of the light innocence of the surfaces on which things are remixed in Lewis Carroll, or the amorphous element that led Heraclitus to declare, "Time is a child playing."

3. Michel Foucault and Maurice Blanchot, *Foucault/Blanchot* (New York: Zone Books, 1987). The idea of *absence d'oeuvre* is the one Derrida at first admired in Foucault. Later he himself would try to distinguish it, and its role in his own thought, from negative theology; similarly of Lacan's *manque* he complains that it stays *à sa place* ("Comment ne pas parler"). Yet Derrida wants to preserve a sort of mystical unrepresentable Law, akin in some ways to Emmanuel Levinas, and so does not want to go all the way to Spinozistic immanence, or the atheist, materialist Jewish tradition with which it is linked (including a whole aspect of Marx). In this regard, Wittgenstein is an interesting case. The "silence" in his early work, linked to his logical atomism, and to Loosian austerity, is in the negative-theological mode, whereas the rambling, deliberately nonexplanatory remarks of the later work move toward an "immanence" of "tacit," disunified rules of language use. As he puts it in the exergue of *Remarks on Psychology*, "I show you the differences."

4. See my "Foucault's Art of Seeing," October 44 (Spring 1988), reprinted in my *Philosophical Events: Essays of the '80s* (New York: Columbia University Press, 1991).

5. Gilles Deleuze, *Francis Bacon: logique de la sensation* (Paris: La Différence, 1981), 57ff.; Deleuze and Guattari repeat this view in *What Is Philosophy?* (New York: Columbia University Press, 1994), where it is connected with another view of monochromes (181ff.).

6. Drawing on the notion introduced by Jean-François Lyotard in his *Discours, figure* (Paris: Klincksieck, 1971), Deleuze opposes "figural" and "figurative" (*Francis Bacon*, 9); thus he says that

Bacon "isolates" his figures from any "figurative" composition, submitting them to another sort of space, whose logic connects to various abstract spaces. The relation with *discours* thus ceases to be "illustrative"—such would be the sense of Bacon's well-known aversion to illustration. In this way Deleuze introduces the notion of a "sensation" of worlds of nonillustratable things. In *What Is Philosophy?* Deleuze and Guattari declare: "Like all painting, abstract painting is sensation, nothing but sensation" (182).

7. Gilles Deleuze and Félix Guattari, *A Thousand Plateaus* (Minneapolis: University of Minnesota Press, 1987), 499.

8. Ibid.

9. This view of series seems to fit with a number of different art practices. In particular in the 1960s one sees the emergence of various serial practices—in pop, where Deleuze, at the time, proposed to see the possibilities of a sort of mad "simulacral" repetition; and in minimalism, where series were used to empty Forms and discover a kind of neutral nonexpressionist "antiform," as with the trance repetitions of minimalist music or the routines of minimalist dance, employing the sorts of strategies that Deleuze analyzes in his study of Beckett's *épuisements*. Benjamin Buchloh also draws attention to series in the work of Gerhard Richter. Starting in the 1960s, Richter would introduce a number of strange new "indifferent" or "neutral" procedures into painting that depart from working from models or motifs and make the question of *how* take precedence over the question of *what* to paint, leading to a particularly large and open oeuvre. In the sixties in analytic philosophy as well, one finds discussion and development of Wittgenstein's problem of following a rule or continuing a series of numbers; one can see Goodman's grue paradox as an example. Thus Saul Kripke generalizes the paradox of possible divergence in continuity in his account of Wittgenstein's skepticism, seeing it as a key to the private-language argument.

10. Preface to Gilles Deleuze and Claire Parnet, *Dialogues* (London: Athlone, 1987), vi. The formula is taken up again in

What Is Philosophy? In his lecture "Bergson and His Critique of Intellectualism," first delivered in Oxford in 1908, William James tries to find a logic that departs at once from the totalities of the British Hegelians and the atoms of Bertrand Russell, seeing such totalities and atoms as "abstractions" from a prior "pluralistic" composition of "things in the making." James's attempt to find a multiple flow of things prior to the "block universe" finds resonance with various views at the time—with Virginia Woolf, for example, and perhaps also with Henri Matisse, who admired Bergson and who invented what Yve-Alain Bois analyzes as a circulation-tension-expansion principle of filling pictorial space, leaving no "holes" and affording a sense of expanded scale. But another sort of Bergsonism is more compatible with holes and *fuites*, connected to contemporary complexity and chaos theory. See Bruno Paradis, "Indétermination et mouvements de bifurcation chez Bergson," *Philosophie* 32 (1991).

11. Deleuze and Parnet, *Dialogues*, viii.

12. Deleuze and Guattari, *A Thousand Plateaus*, 511.

13. See "Bergsonism"; and, on the concept of the virtual, Gilles Deleuze, *Différence et répétition* (Paris: Presses Universitaires de France, 1968), 269ff.

14. Deleuze and Guattari, *A Thousand Plateaus*, 511.

15. Gilles Deleuze, *Pourparlers* (Paris: Minuit, 1990), 64ff.

16. Ibid., 84; cf. also 73ff.

17. Lessing's doctrine of the separation of the senses, and in particular of eye from ear, belongs with what Foucault analyzes in *The Order of Things* (New York: Pantheon, 1971) as a "classical space," preceded by a "complicated" Neoplatonism and a baroque. For Deleuze, one might add that such classical representation is followed as well by a modernity captured in Klee's remark that to again see movement in painting as in the universe, he had to rid himself of Lessing's misguided separations. At one point Deleuze thus refers to what Rimbaud called the *dérèglement des sens*. Deleuze is talking about the "modernity" of Kant. In his view, it is not that Kantian "self-criticism" points the

way to what is "modern" or "modernist" in art; rather, through the notion of an "unregulated" (*déréglé*) use of faculties in its connection with two other "poetic formulas" ("Je suis un autre," and "the time is out of joint") Kant's philosophy opens to a modernity he did not yet imagine. See "On Four Poetic Formulas Which Might Summarize the Kantian Philosophy," in *Kant's Critical Philosophy: The Doctrine of Faculties* (Minneapolis: University of Minnesota Press, 1984), xi ff.

18. Deleuze, *Francis Bacon*, 69. Rosalind Krauss has elaborated the link between "formless" space and the floor or *sol* in Pollock in an original manner. See her *The Optical Unconscious* (Cambridge: MIT Press, 1993).

19. Bernard Cache, *Earth Moves* (Cambridge: MIT Press, 1995).

20. Deleuze and Guattari, *A Thousand Plateaus*, 497.

21. Ibid.

22. One might try to associate this distinction between a figurative geometric abstraction and a prior, more "topographical" one with certain passages in the modern philosophical discussions of geometry. There is Wittgenstein's attempt to rid himself of the "Platonic" view that geometric forms are ideal entities against which reality is compared (or from which they would be "abstracted") and to see geometric and "ordinary" forms instead as quite incomparable, belonging to different language games. There is also the problem of the "origin of geometry" in Husserl analyzed by the young Derrida and connected to certain nongeometric notions of "force." As with the young Derrida, Deleuze finds such "baroque" force in Leibniz; but he connects it as well with models that depart from the sets and functions dear to Frege and Russell to describe things like continuous variation or topological points of singularity. For a critical discussion of this view, see Alain Badiou, "The Fold, Leibniz and the Baroque," in *Gilles Deleuze and the Theater of Philosophy*, ed. Constantin V. Boundas and Dorothea Olkowski (London: Routledge, 1994). On the possible impact of such "dynamic" nonrectilinear models in architecture, see Greg Lynn, "New Variations on the Rowe Complex," *ANY* 7/8 (September/October 1994).

23. See Mark Johnson, *The Body in the Mind* (Chicago: University of Chicago Press, 1987). Today one might see Johnson as part of a phenomenological reaction to the "functionalist" thesis (the mind as brain program), to which Hilary Putnam, changing his mind, also comes to object. For his part Deleuze looks at how the phenomenological theme of the "flesh" (in which "the mind" would be incarnated) took art or aesthetics as a privileged domain; in particular, he admires Henri Maldiney. Yet Deleuze finds the idea of "the flesh," with its religious overtones, to be rather too *tender* and so lacking the mad noncognitive *violence* of the visual that one sees for example in Bacon.

24. Stan Allen finds another, more "cinematic" logic in Le Corbusier than the official "mechanical" one, linked to certain "light" features of contemporary architecture; see "Le Corbusier and Modernist Movement," *ANY* 5 (March/April 1994). Similarly, perhaps someone will find another, more "Jamesian" or "Bergsonian" logic in Frank Lloyd Wright than the official organicist one.

25. See Gilles Deleuze, "Mediators," in *Zone 6: Incorporations*, ed. Jonathan Crary and Sanford Kwinter (Cambridge: MIT Press, 1992). The same kind of problem concerning the fate of "abstract thought" in politics is taken up in discussion with Toni Negri, where Deleuze declares: "To believe in the world, that is what we most lack; we have completely lost the world, it has been taken from us." *Pourparlers*, 239.

26. Or, in Gerhard Richter's words in a well-known interview with Benjamin Buchloh, the aim is "to bring together in a living and viable way the most different and the most contradictory elements in the greatest possible freedom. Not paradise."

Five Grounds

This essay first appeared as "Some Senses of Grounding," in *Anybody*, ed. Cynthia Davidson (Cambridge: MIT Press, 1997).

1. An important source (if not the ground) for such analogies comes from the translation of *ratio* by *Grund*, though of course the *logos* of which *ratio* is the translation already implies a

geospatial language. Some scholars attribute this philosophical use of the term *Grund* to women mystics at the time of Meister Eckhart (thirteenth century), whose "visions" could not be said in Latin, since women couldn't know that language. In any case *Grund* was to become an important word in philosophy with a life of its own, seen for example in Heidegger's book on Leibniz called *Der Satz von dem Grund* (The Essence of Reasons). Two destinies of the term in modern philosophy fit my exercise. One is Heidegger's play with the word *Abgrund* (abyss), notably in his study of Nietzsche, later taken up by Derrida, who identifies "deconstructive" with "abyssal" readings. The other is Deleuze's neologism *effondement* (ungrounding) in *Différence et répétition* (Paris: Presses Universitaires de France, 1968). Here *Grund* is *fond*, as with the relations *forme/fond* (figure/ground). Deleuze's ungrounding is not an "abyss making"; it is the emergence of an "intensive space" prior to any *extensio* divisible *partes ex partibus*, which traces another sort of relation to *forme* or figure (229–232). Deleuze wants to extract the sense of "ground" from the notions of "reason" or "logos," and in particular from Leibniz's principle of sufficient reason (*Grund*). He points to a "layer of sense" prior to the "reasons" or "grounds" of things and says that precisely in this stratum does thought live and die, confronting the stupidity that it must combat (272–277). One consequence is that abstraction or "nonrepresentation" can be understood in a new way: in terms of ungrounding. *Effondement* releases a dynamic "abstract line" that no longer moves within figure/ground relations as in the case of abstraction that is content to simply reduce or purify away figures from a basically immobile, rectilinear extensive space.

2. See the critical edition that includes Wölfflin's notes in *Empathy, Form, and Space: Problems in German Aesthetics 1873–1893*, trans. Harry Francis Mallgrave and Eleftherios Ikonomou (Santa Monica: Getty Center for the History of Art and the Humanities, 1994).

3. Le Corbusier, *The Radiant City* (New York: Orion Press, 1967), 55–56.

4. It is Deleuze who first introduces Hamlet's phrase "the time is out of joint" in a philosophical context—as the first of "four poetic formulas which might summarize the Kantian philosophy"; see the preface to *Kant's Critical Philosophy* (Minneapolis: University of Minnesota Press, 1984). In the revised French version, *Critique et clinique* (Paris: Minuit, 1993), 40ff., he adds a historical note about how this notion of time out of joint differs from the temporal "aberrations" that one finds in ancient meteorological or terrestrial notions of time, which still stay within the circles or spirals of determinant movement. "Time out of joint" is "the time of the city and nothing else," he declares (42)—it no longer depends on an original cosmic movement of the heavens nor on a rural movement of seasons or weather. Perhaps it remains a time in our "global cities," where the distinction between artifice and nature tends to be blurred in at least the sense suggested below.

5. Dan Graham, "Gordon Matta-Clark," in *Gordon Matta Clark* (Valencia: IVAM Centre Julio Gonzalez, 1993), 378–380.

6. See the section on entropy in Yve-Alain Bois and Rosalind Krauss, *L'informe: mode d'emploi* (Paris: Centre Pompidou, 1996). In architecture, Krauss sees Matta-Clark continued by Rem Koolhaas. Thus she declares that "Koolhaas's position that the scale of contemporary architectural projects (like the Bibliothèque de France) is beyond design as we have thought of it before" leads him to questions of "formlessness and disorientation"; by contrast, Frank Gehry in his recent museum projects only "makes artily elaborate concatenations of different elements" (*ANY* 5, March/April 1994). Similarly Koolhaas is prepared to count Matta-Clark as an unintended precursor of his "strategy of the void" in the Big Library, although without the "glamour of violation" first associated with Matta-Clark or with Lucio Fontana in painting ("Thinking Big," *Artforum* 33 [December 1994], 46–65). The delight in "violation" in Matta-Clark's work is often associated with his attempt to open private spaces to public spectacle in politically charged settings; and in his work with the Anarchitecture Group, he was involved with introducing voids or gaps in urban "movement space" that might serve to

interrupt daily routines. But what happens to such "violation" in Koolhaas's "big" design? When for example Krauss likens the library to Giacometti's X, the comparison seems primarily morphological or "sculptural"; see "Six Notes on the Subject of the Grid," in *Anyone*, ed. Cynthia Davidson (New York: Rizzoli, 1991). Yet for the connection to be *only* of this sort would seem to weaken the force of her contrast with Gehry's mere "decoration."

7. Cf. Gilles Deleuze, *Francis Bacon: logique de la sensation* (Paris: La Différence, 1981); and for the relation between face and ground in classical Albertian tradition, see the plateau on "faciality" in Gilles Deleuze and Félix Guattari, *A Thousand Plateaus* (Minneapolis: University of Minnesota Press, 1987). In describing the "figures" in Bacon's paintings Deleuze refers to a distinction drawn by Jean-François Lyotard in his book *Discours, figure* (Paris: Klincksieck, 1971) between "figural" and "figurative" space. The latter is in effect the space of Alberti while the former replaces the vanishing point with an invisible "matrix." In figural space, the body would discover the "plasticity" seen in Bacon's paintings, which Deleuze contrasts with the still-too-pious phenomenological conception of the "flesh." Thus one may count Bacon's "figures" as an instance of what below I call the "indefiniteness" of the spatial body. Deleuze and Guattari draw on literary examples in their discussion of faciality, notably the moment in Proust when the face becomes *défaite* (undone). One may thus link the indeterminateness of the body in Bacon's pictorial figures with its role in relation to literary figures or personae—one example would be Herman Melville's idea of such figures as "originals" (see Deleuze, *Critique et clinique*, 106ff.).

8. Quoted in "Paul Virilio and the Oblique," introduced by Enrique Limon, in *Sites & Stations, Provisional Utopias* ed. Stan Allen with Kyong Park, *Bau* 13 (Madrid), and *Arch + 2* (April 1996).

9. Ibid. On Virilio's relations with *Gestalttheorie* and Merleau-Ponty, hence with figure/ground relations, see Paul Virilio, *Cybermonde, la politique du pire: entretien avec Philippe Petit* (Paris: Textuel, 1996), 23ff. For Deleuze's view of the limitations of Gestalt theory, cf. Gilles Deleuze and Félix Guattari, *What Is Philosophy?* (New York: Columbia University Press, 1994), 208ff.

10. Ibid.

11. One finds such ideas in the "philosophies of indetermination" that move from Bergson to James and to Whitehead, James correcting "psychology" and Whitehead "cosmology" so as to make room for them. Thus Bergson talked about an "open society" long before Karl Popper and in a different sense—a society is open when based not on myths and origins but on differences and "fabulations." It would be instructive to reread Georges Sorel's *Illusions of Progress* and *Reflections on Violence* of 1908 in this light, as well as the sociology of George Herbert Mead. In a more contemporary vein, Gilles Châtelet offers a sharp critique of the current enthusiasm for "self-organizing systems," opposing to them a model of *l'homme quelconque*—one might say a model of "anybody" in the indefinite or indeterminate sense sketched below. Cf. "Du chaos et de l'auto-organisation comme néo-conservatisme festif," *Les Temps Modernes* 581 (March-April 1995).

12. Cf. Saskia Sassen, "Whose City Is It? Globalization and the Formation of New Claims," *Public Culture* 8, no. 2 (Winter 1996).

13. On this sense of "indefiniteness," cf. Gilles Deleuze "L'immanence: une vie," *Philosophie* 47 (1995), 5.

Six Other Geometries

This essay was first given as a lecture at a conference on "other geometries" held on the occasion of the opening of Peter Eisenman's Aronoff Center in Cincinnati, Ohio.

1. Gilles Deleuze, "Michel Tournier or the World without the Other," in *The Logic of Sense* (New York: Columbia University Press, 1990); the theme is taken up in *Difference and Repetition* (New York: Columbia University Press, 1994), 281–282, and in Gilles Deleuze and Félix Guattari, *What Is Philosophy?* (New York: Columbia University Press, 1994), 16–19.

2. Michel Tournier, *Friday* (New York: Pantheon, 1985); cf. Deleuze's analysis in *The Logic of Sense*.

3. Gilles Deleuze and Félix Guattari, *A Thousand Plateaus* (Minneapolis: University of Minnesota Press, 1987), 167–191. On the problem of the face in Proust and Melville, see ibid., 185ff., where there is a question of the face becoming "undone" (*défaite*: "disaggregate" in the translation). Something like the face undone is what Deleuze sees in Bacon.

4. That is Deleuze's argument in *Francis Bacon: logique de la sensation* (Paris: La Différence, 1981).

5. Gilles Deleuze starts this analysis already in *Proust and Signs* (New York: Braziller, 1972).

6. Gilles Deleuze, "Bartleby ou la formule," in *Critique et clinique* (Paris: Minuit, 1993), 89–114; on the problem of identity and "the highway" see "Whitman," in ibid., 73–80.

7. Michel Serres, *Le système de Leibniz et ses modèles mathématiques* (Paris: Presses Universitaires de France, 1968).

8. On Wittgenstein's work on his sister's villa, see Paul Wijdeveld, *Ludwig Wittgenstein, Architect* (Cambridge: MIT Press, 1994). In his remarks on mathematics, he derives the problem of "following a rule" from the problem of continuity— what it means to continue a series of numbers. But Wittgenstein doesn't consider the case of the sort of "irrational" continuity that, for example, Deleuze associates with Godard's montage, which derives from the connection between interstitial spaces and the open whole; cf. Gilles Deleuze, *L'image-temps* (Paris: Minuit, 1985), 233ff. Here the problem of "rules" and their formulations is understood in relation to an unregulated (nonprobabilistic) sort of chance—in the case of Godard, associated with the "virtual" film image.

9. *Edmund Husserl's Origins of Geometry: An Introduction*, with a commentary by Jacques Derrida (Stony Brook, N.Y.: N. Hays, 1978). For Deleuze's remarks on this work, see Deleuze and Guattari, *A Thousand Plateaus*, 367ff.

10. Greg Lynn, "New Variations on the Rowe Complex," *ANY* 7/8 (September/October 1994).

11. In "The Intellectual Sheik" (*ANY* 7/8, September/October 1994), Peter Eisenman offers a more complicated view of this turn in Rowe's work—we oughtn't to see it as a turn from architecture to urbanism or from formalism to historicism but rather as a move from an "abstract" to an "empiricist" kind of formalism. For Eisenman, Rowe remains a formalist, his disappointment with Le Corbusier deriving from a sensed lack in the "transformative power" of the architect's "formal mechanisms." But this is just the problem with Rowe. In both phases he seeks in "internal form" a neutrality with respect to ideology, while in neither case is such a moral stance in fact possible. A variant on this reading might start with Eisenman's observation that Rowe's literal/phenomenal, figure/ground distinctions fit better with the "Gestaltist aspects of phenomenology in Husserl and Merleau-Ponty" than Rowe's English attitudes would allow; and that other kinds of "formal possibilities" belonging to neither of Rowe's phases are thus to be found in certain philosophical attempts to go beyond that phenomenological framework. We have already seen such an attempt in Deleuze's view of the problems of *autrui* and of "minor geometries"; the contrast with respect to Gestaltist views is developed in his distinction between "intensive" and "extensive" space (*Difference and Repetition*, 228ff.). My suggestion below is that we associate this notion of "intensive space" with an opposition not between "abstract" and "empiricist" but rather between "reductive" and "operative" form. What then happens to the moral argument about "neutrality" that apparently motivates Rowe, along with Eisenman's own changing attitudes to it?

12. Jean-François Lyotard, *Discours, figure* (Paris: Klincksieck, 1971).

13. Rem Koolhaas, "Typical Plan," in *S, M, L, XL* (New York: Monacelli Press, 1996), 334ff.

Seven **Future Cities**

This essay will appear in *(In)Visible Cities* (forthcoming from the Monacelli Press).

1. All figures are taken from *World Resources, 1996–97: A Guide to the Global Environment* (New York: Oxford University Press, 1996).

2. I discuss "Foucault's art of seeing" in my *Philosophical Events: Essays of the '80s* (New York: Columbia University Press, 1991), 68ff.

Eight **The Virtual House**

This essay first appeared in *ANY* 19/20 (September/October 1997).

1. See, for example, Gilles Deleuze, *Différence et répétition* (Paris: Presses Universitaires de France, 1968), 269ff.

Index of Names